# GLOBAL FINANCE

Written under the shadow of the global financial crisis, this book charts the current shape of global finance and tries to explain why the crisis arose – and what can be done about it. Economics alone cannot fully explain how global finance operates, and why it is so crisis prone. *Global Finance* offers a wider approach in three key ways, by:

- setting markets and financial market failure in a historical context
- bringing politics and culture back into the analysis of global finance
- drawing on the latest thinking by sociologists of economic life.

With a convincing argument for better regulation of markets, Robert Holton provides a fascinating insight into the volatile and often misunderstood world of global finance. This is a key text for undergraduate students of sociology, economics, business, and politics, as well as being an incisive, informative read for anyone with an interest in this topical issue.

**Robert J. Holton** is Professor Emeritus in Sociology at Trinity College, Dublin, and Adjunct Professor of Sociology at Flinders University of South Australia. His publications include *Globalization and the Nation-State* (2011), *Cosmopolitanisms: New Thinking and New Directions* (2009), *Global Networks* (2008), and *Making Globalization* (2005).

# SHORTCUTS – 'Little Books on Big Issues'

*Shortcuts* is a major new series of concise, accessible introductions to some of the major issues of our times. The series is developed as an A to Z coverage of emergent or new social, cultural and political phenomena. Issues and topics covered range from Google to global finance, from climate change to the new capitalism, from Blogs to the future of books. Whilst the principal focus of *Shortcuts* is the relevance of current issues, topics, debates and thinkers to the social sciences and humanities, the books should also appeal to a wider audience seeking guidance on how to engage with today's leading social, political and philosophical debates.

**Series Editor**: Anthony Elliott is a social theorist, writer and Chair in the Department of Sociology at Flinders University, Australia. He is also Visiting Research Professor in the Department of Sociology at the Open University, UK, and Visiting Professor in the Department of Sociology at University College Dublin, Ireland. His writings have been published in sixteen languages, and he has written widely on, amongst other topics, identity, globalization, society, celebrity, and mobilities.

Titles in the series:

**Confronting Climate Change**
*Constance Lever-Tracy*

**Feelings**
*Stephen Frosh*

**Suicide Bombings**
*Riaz Hassan*

**Web 2.0**
*Sam Han*

**Freedom**
*Nick Stevenson*

**Global Finance**
*Robert J. Holton*

# GLOBAL FINANCE

*Robert J. Holton*

Routledge
Taylor & Francis Group

LONDON AND NEW YORK

First published 2012
by Routledge
2 Park Square, Milton Park, Abingdon, Oxon OX14 4RN

Simultaneously published in the USA and Canada
by Routledge
711 Third Avenue, New York, NY 10017

*Routledge is an imprint of the Taylor & Francis Group, an informa
business*

© 2012 Robert J. Holton

The right of Robert J. Holton to be identified as author of this
work has been asserted by him in accordance with the Copyright,
Designs and Patents Act 1988.

*British Library Cataloguing in Publication Data*
A catalogue record for this book is available from the British
Library

*Library of Congress Cataloging-in-Publication Data*
A catalog record for this book has been requested

ISBN: 978-0-415-61916-5 (hbk)
ISBN: 978-0-415-61917-2 (pbk)
ISBN: 978-0-203-82840-3 (ebk)

Typeset in Bembo
by Taylor & Francis Books

MIX
Paper from
responsible sources
FSC
www.fsc.org
FSC® C004839

Printed and bound in Great Britain by
TJ International Ltd, Padstow, Cornwall

# CONTENTS

*Series editor's preface*                                          vi
*Preface*                                                          vii

1   Global finance                                         1

2   Global finance: what it is and how it operates          8

3   The history and social geography of global finance      34

4   The social actors in global finance: market culture and
    financial knowledge                            55

5   Society and finance: an alternative theoretical
    approach                                        71

6   Global finance and public policy                        85

*Glossary*                                                         107
*Further reading*                                                  110
*Web resources*                                                    112
*Index*                                                            114

# SERIES EDITOR'S PREFACE

## SHORTCUTS – '*Little Books on Big Issues*'

*Anthony Elliott*

*Shortcuts* is a major new series of concise, accessible introductions to some of the major issues of our times. The series is developed as an A to Z coverage of emergent or new social, cultural and political phenomena. Issues and topics covered range from Google to global finance, from climate change to the new capitalism, from Blogs to the future of books. Whilst the principal focus of *Shortcuts* is the relevance of current issues, topics and debates to the social sciences and humanities, the books should also appeal to a wider audience seeking guidance on how to engage with today's leading social, political, and philosophical debates.

The advent of the global electronic economy is in many ways synonymous with change, and perhaps nowhere more clearly so than as a result of the global financial crisis of 2008 and beyond. Toxic assets, crippled bank balance sheets, the implosion of share markets, the collapse of some of the biggest names on Wall Street, the disintegration of national economies and the worldwide shrinkage in employment and consumerism: this is the heady cocktail of explosive socio-economic forces analysed with great sociological ingenuity and erudition by Robert Holton. In *Global Finance*, Holton examines with impressive theoretical sensitivity the rise of finance capital which reaches beyond national forms of organization. Beyond the current roller coaster of crisis, default and financial loss, Holton sets out a brilliant argument for the better regulation of markets. The book is a wonderful shortcut to an alternative global future for global finance.

# PREFACE

## Global finance: the argument

This book is written under the shadow of the global financial crisis. It sets out to chart the current shape of global finance, to explain why the crisis arose, and what can be done about it. Economics alone cannot fully explain how global finance operates and why it is so crisis prone. A wider approach is offered. This sets markets and financial market failure in a historical context. It also brings politics and culture back into the analysis of global finance, including new ways of understanding how and why financial traders, bankers, and regulators act as they do, and why the legitimacy of global finance is under such threat from public opinion. This draws on the latest thinking by sociologists of economic life, who have identified dysfunctional aspects of markets based on narrow conceptions of self-interest and market equilibrium.

Global finance is primarily concerned with markets for credit that cross political boundaries. Households, business, and states all borrow extensively to meet their needs, with financial institutions mediating between investors and borrowers. Crisis, default, and financial loss is not, however, new, but has a long history. This reflects the high risks and uncertainties that surround financial transactions based on promises of future repayment – risks that markets and most economic observers repeatedly fail to take account of. Markets, like many other systems, are prone to extreme events, highly damaging in their consequences, yet unrecognized in economic thought.

The historical recurrence of global financial crises over the last 200 years, is also fundamentally linked with utopian beliefs that markets can be self-correcting and self-regulating. Rethinking the place of markets in society is, however, bedevilled by a tendency to think in terms of two broad options – either free markets or highly regulated command economies. This book argues for a need to go beyond this dichotomy if any progress is to be made in understanding and reducing the volatility of financial markets. State policies and regulatory arrangements failed in the lead up to the global financial crisis but so did 'free' markets. Neither option is adequate by itself. What is required is better regulation of markets, and a more productive relationship between markets and democratic debate.

It is dysfunctional for social cohesion to allow markets excessive autonomy. In the concluding section of the book, new rules and norms are outlined that can better regulate financial markets while avoiding excessively authoritarian forms of state control.

# 1

# GLOBAL FINANCE

This book is intended to make sense of global finance. There can be few topics of such immediate importance, whether to citizens, businesses, or governments. The recent global financial crisis (GFC), which began in 2007, is still playing out in the sovereign debt crisis of a number of European countries and the USA, while many global banks remain subject to stress tests to determine whether they would withstand further financial shocks if conditions deteriorate. Citizens find they are paying many of the costs of financial breakdown whether through unemployment, cuts to public services or increased taxation, while many businesses are finding credit hard to obtain. So how is it that this situation has arisen and what can be done about it?

Global finance has an enormous dynamic potential, yet its economic power and global scope raise fundamental challenges to national sovereignty, democratic politics, and international co-operation. These challenges are magnified by the problems of risk and severe economic instability to which the sector is prone, posing further challenges for global as well as national public policy as to how global finance is best regulated.

Many discussions of global finance are written by economists and management specialists, and others by financial regulators or journalists. The distinctiveness of the present study, written by a sociologist and economic historian, is that it takes a rather different and far broader approach. This has two main features. First, it places global finance within society and subject to political and cultural as well as economic processes. Second, it is historical and as such not limited to the present or to immediate financial concerns.

Economics does not provide all the answers to an understanding of how global finance works, while a focus exclusively on the present does not engage with the historical fact that global finance and globalization itself has a long history. Financial crises are not new but endemic to market-based economic systems. Much of the rhythm of global finance over the last 300 years has been cyclical in nature, as Charles Kindleberger famously pointed out in *Manias, Panics and Crashes* (1978). Such cycles followed a pattern of credit expansion–speculation–bubble–distress–bust. Many look to economists for answers to these questions, but there is equally a strong sense that economics failed to predict crisis and may only have limited purchase on its causes. The alternative sociological approach outlined in this book includes greater emphasis both on historical trends and instabilities in global finance, and gives close attention to the cultural worlds of finance, to the traders and bankers at the heart of the system. The idea that markets work simply through the rational pursuit of self-interest is too simplistic and needs to be replaced by a broader sense of the culture, social psychology, emotions, and discursive contours of financial market players. These shed light on how markets work, and why participants fundamentally underestimated risks and uncertainties, leading eventually to crisis.

Markets and financial institutions, together with investors, borrowers and savers, are then part of wider social arrangements, rather than operating in an entirely separate economic domain. This does not mean economic thought is not helpful or productive. Indeed, economic theory acts not simply as a commentary on economic life, but also helps to shape the way economic activity is organized. The problem is rather that economics, as we shall see, is not enough if we want to understand how markets work. There is, after all, a two-way flow of influences between the economy, on the one hand, and political, legal, and cultural processes on the other. Such processes include public regulation of markets, legislation and legal norms concerning economic property rights, and acceptable forms of economic transaction, as well as cultural expectations and conventions concerning the purposes, functioning, and limits to the scope of economic activity. Markets have, in other words, social, political, and cultural preconditions as well as consequences. They are acted out or performed by individuals and groups according to ways of understanding economic life, that arise within the broader social infrastructures that markets inhabit. This is true both within nations and in cross-border activities where differences in political arrangements, legal requirements, and cultural practices affect how business is done. Research in areas such as management styles, modes of negotiation, and preferred forms of legal regulation show this to be the case.

So while the ideal of 'free' markets is widespread, it would be misleading to assume that this amounts to a complete description of how markets actually work. Finance markets may appear impersonal, a characteristic enhanced both by the extensive use of computer-based transactions and by the secretive nature of confidential business practice. Yet they are performed by individuals operating within organizations and networks. Market participants must make judgements not simply about price signals and what they mean for investment, saving, employment, and consumption, but also about who they trust, what operating methods are legitimate, how they interpret risk, what legal and political obligations are required of them, and whether ethical considerations should enter into market behaviour. This does not mean that market participants necessarily comply with external norms and obligations – tax evasion and insider share dealing being two obvious areas where they do not. But it does mean that there is a wider social setting to be reckoned with. Even if self-interest or greed are the norm, there are circumstances – such as repeated financial crises over the last 300 years – where they are inadequate as guides to behaviour, and where the location of markets within society can no longer be ignored.

This is evident in the emergence of criticism over the legitimacy of high salaries and bonuses paid to financiers who have presided over banking failure. It is also connected with arguments that businesses that receive massive public bail-outs in order to survive financial collapse should not simply carry on as before, but should have a greater public responsibility for their actions. The wider social and political context is also reflected in adverse commentary on the widespread tendency of banks to raise their own interest rates in excess of central bank interest rate rises. Legislators and regulators, as well as citizens, take these matters seriously and often seek redress. Whereas conventional economic thought brackets out much of this wider array of concerns and influences, in this book they are brought back in to the analysis.

The development of global finance is part and parcel of wider social arrangements, but it is equally connected with that much-hyped and omnipresent phenomenon of globalization. This involves a growth and intensification in cross-border transactions and relationships, such that the world becomes increasingly interdependent. This interdependence is seen within an international division of labour which sees raw materials, manufactured goods, and financial services exported and imported. But it also applies to finance, where money markets for investment capital, foreign exchange, government debt, real estate, and household consumption depend on global linkages between borrowers and investors, conducted through financial intermediaries. Nations may have particular profiles in terms of the types and scale of financial institutions located within them, levels of domestic savings, and levels of public expenditure and debt. Yet their room for manoeuvre in financial matters is circumscribed by the integration of national finance within global arrangements. Such limits apply even to the world's largest and most powerful nation, the USA, whose deficits both in international trade and in government expenditure depend on huge inflows of global capital, including massive purchase by China of US government bonds. Without these global inflows, US consumers would have to curtail their consumption, corporations would have to limit capital expenditure, and governments would have to slash public spending.

Global interdependence also means that events or crises in one region spill over to many others. This happened in the Wall Street crash of 1929 and subsequent Great Depression. It has also happened in the recent financial crisis. The reverberations of this renewed episode of global financial dislocation have been felt not only in the USA where banking collapse and the sub-prime mortgage crisis bit deepest, or in Europe where banking crisis has been combined with sovereign debt crises and political instability in smaller countries such as Greece and Ireland. The crisis also has ramifications for Latin America, Africa, and Asia, as the upward trajectory in the growth in world trade faltered, while global capital markets reduced the supply of credit and largely abandoned poorer indebted nations.

Economic globalization involves cross-border trade, investment, migration, and technology transfer. These are associated not simply with cross-border flows of economic activity and interdependence, but also with evolving power structures that contain within them significant global inequalities, as well as challenging older understandings of national sovereignty. Nation-states, as recent events in Europe indicate, have to deal with the global financial system, because they typically need to borrow money internationally to finance budget deficits. The sovereign debts involved arise from the sale of government bonds to investors, but the prices which investors are prepared to pay to hold bonds reflect private calculations and perceptions of the creditworthiness of nations. The more risky, the higher the interest rate investors demand, posing further challenges to the finances of the states involved, and to their freedom of manoeuvre in setting levels and deciding types of government spending. These in turn challenge the idea that nation-states should be self-governing according to democratic principles. So while the operations of multi-national companies were the focus of earlier debates over the challenges of the global economy to nations and democracy, this focus has recently shifted to a new preoccupation with bond markets and the fiscal challenges facing ostensibly self-governing nations. National sovereignty and global bond markets seem to be incompatible with each other, with democracy a further casualty in the process.

The place of global finance within economic globalization has also been growing. Thus the massive upswing in economic globalization that has taken place over the last two decades saw an increase in the relative importance of finance within the global economy, as compared with manufacturing and primary production. This change has been associated both with a massive increase in the global scale and outreach of banks and other financial institutions and with the volume and complexity of financial transactions within the global economy. Major players in global finance now include hedge funds and private equity funds as well as banks and insurance companies, while new instruments such as derivatives have grown up alongside bonds, shares, loans, and mortgages.

Global finance, then, is not simply a matter of institutions and products, but also of the people and occupational groups that constitute financial markets, together with the ideas and forms of knowledge that guide and influence their actions. Its operation depends both on this internal set of activities and on a wider set of social and political influences. These are the guiding perspectives of this study, which is organized as follows.

## Plan of the book

In Chapter 2, attention is focused on what exactly global finance is and how it operates. This provides an account of the underlying principles of finance and credit, as well as an account of the leading institutions and products involved in the global financial arena. These include the growth of securitization and derivatives, together with new developments in investment banking around arbitrage. These important technical terms are explained in non-technical language. The chapter also identifies the paradox that global finance is simultaneously very creative and at the same time so destructive. These are characteristics that the Austrian economic historian Joseph Schumpeter saw as fundamental to capitalism itself.

Attention turns in Chapter 3 to the history and social geography of global finance, including questions as to the origins of global finance, and its evolving spatial location within the global economy. This identifies the historical origins and key moments in the evolution of global finance, whose history goes back millennia, and the spatial locations in which global finance has operated. Attention is also given to structures of financial power, referred to by many recent commentators as financialization, and what they mean for the place of finance within the economy as a whole. Finally, the evidence for historical patterns of boom, bust, upswing, and crisis, is reviewed, breaking down the general idea of financial crisis into distinct types and considering how far the GFC has taken on new dimensions.

Chapter 4 looks at a neglected feature of global finance, namely the cultural worlds of global finance and the key players involved. This examines the importance of new information technology and electronic trading, while being equally concerned with the social dynamics of trading rooms and deliberations by central bankers. The emotions and social psychology of global finance are discussed as a means of enriching accounts of economic life beyond the impoverished assumptions of rational self-interest.

Chapter 5 brings together the case for grounding the study of finance markets within a broad sociological approach. While there have been many criticisms of the narrow focus of conventional economics in the past, these have not displaced economics as the place analysts go to find answers to economic challenges and to the reasons for GFC. In this chapter, the values underlying support for markets are discussed, and in particular the attractions of utopian projections of markets as systems of natural liberty. This market utopianism, rather than any superior analytical capacity, is argued to be the main obstacle to a shift toward a sociological approach to economic life, embracing culture and politics.

Chapter 6 turns to more practical issues to do with public policy and whether global finance can be made to work better. This examines attempts to address the instabilities and risks associated with global finance through a re-structuring of global financial architecture, and whether these are likely to be successful. Attention is also given to problems of a democracy deficit in the area of global finance and how this might be addressed. Global finance has an enormous dynamic potential, yet its economic power and global scope raise fundamental challenges to national sovereignty, democratic politics, and international co-operation. These challenges are magnified by the problems of risk and severe economic instability to which the sector is prone, posing further challenges for global as well as national public policy as to how global finance is best regulated.

# 2

# GLOBAL FINANCE

## What it is and how it operates

This chapter is organized around the following questions. What exactly does global finance entail? What are the key institutions involved, and how do they operate?

## Introduction

Global finance, as we have seen, stands at the intersection of two broad long-term processes. One is the development of specialist financial institutions serving households, businesses, and states. The other is globalization: a complex set of processes involving cross-border flows and dependencies arising from not only the mobility of capital, commodities, technology, and people, but also political ideas and institutions, and cultural ways of life. Without global finance it is unlikely that economic globalization would be sustainable. However, it is equally the case that repeated global financial crises are evident across history, raising questions about why it is that global finance bears with it a high level of risk, and whether such crises can be avoided in the future.

Global finance is a familiar feature of contemporary life that may be identified with a range of businesses, markets, and public institutions. These span banking, insurance, and investment, products such as shares, bonds, loans of various kinds including mortgages, and more complex financial instruments such as derivatives including futures – all of which will be explored further below. They involve well-known banking giants such as Goldman Sachs and Barclays, insurance businesses such as Lloyds, hedge funds such as JP Morgan Chase or Soros Fund Management, less well-known bond dealers such as Pimco, debt ratings agencies such as Moodys and Standard and Poors, and a range of trading markets. These include face-to-face 'open outcry' markets such as the New York Stock Exchange and the Chicago Board of Trade (which trades commodities and bonds), and electronic screen-based markets such as the Nasdaq – US share dealing markets specializing in high-tech companies – or the vast electronic global foreign exchange markets. These markets are centred in global cities, not only New York, London, and Chicago, but also Tokyo, Sydney, and Zurich.

Recent economic globalization in combination with new communications and information technologies has meant that global finance never sleeps. Trading is spread across a global twenty-four-hour period, meaning that a succession of market centres open and close across a range of different time-zones. Electronic communication involves special trading and information screens displaying a constant stream of market information delivered by specialist terminals from news providers such as Bloomberg and Reuters.

And beyond this rather breathless world of global dealing based on constantly changing market prices and commercial news is the slower but equally globally connected world of central banks and regulators. Some of these are organized internationally such as the Bank for International Settlements, some regionally such as the European Central Bank, some nationally such as the US Federal Reserve or Bank of England, and some on a sub-national basis, such as regulatory agencies in the various US states. Making the picture even more complicated are private organizations that are charged with regulating specific industry sectors within global finance, such as the International Swaps and Derivatives Association, or the International Association of Investment Bankers.

## Some general preconditions of global finance

Before we look in detail at financial processes and institutions, it is important to place finance markets in a broader social and political setting. Such markets may seem, at first, to more or less organize themselves, balancing supply and demand through price mechanisms. On this view one would expect that analysis of the functioning of markets can be left to economics. Yet to assume this view of finance begs many important questions. How is it, for example, that various markets arise in the first place, especially those involving highly mobile and highly risky kinds of transactions? Why and how, in particular, have cross-border markets for capital and credit arisen, when there is no absolute guarantee that loans will be repaid to banks, that share prices will remain buoyant, and that bond-holders will continue to receive regular interest payments from corporations or governments? And why is it that public confidence in finance in general and global finance in particular is so volatile, including periods of extreme suspicion and criticism such as the present? In following through these kinds of questions, a broader enquiry drawing on wider resources in social science is required.

Sociology, in particular, has developed a suitably broad way of understanding markets and economic globalization, which examines the ways in which social and economic activities and institutions interact and influence each other. The theoretical basis for this strand of thinking is explored in more depth in Chapter 5. For the moment we note the particular language in which much of this approach proceeds. This speaks both of the embedding of the economy in society and of the periodic dis-embedding of markets from wider social regulation. An alternative, more familiar, way of describing dis-embedding is to speak of de-regulation. But underlying these analytical questions is one of the central public policy questions of our time. Should markets be left free of intervention to generate maximum economic welfare? Or is public regulation of markets (and finance markets most of all) necessary to prevent recurrent crises, promote stability of investment and employment, and better manage risk?

This study adopts the broader sociological approach, namely, that finance markets characterized by highly mobile flows of capital and sources of credit do not emerge spontaneously, but have to be created, recreated, and often reformed. One reason for this involves high levels of political and cultural hostility found throughout history to characteristic features of money markets. These include the lending of money in return for interest (usury), seen as immoral and prohibited by many religions. Similar resistance has been expressed to financial speculation, where speculators have no underlying interest in the resource or asset whose price is receiving speculative attention. Other more general resistances include hostility to market determination of the prices of necessities such as food and fuel, seen especially when supplies run short and prices rise steeply unless controlled by political authorities. So while markets have a long history, this has usually seen regulation of various kinds, ranging from the administrative control of prices to prohibitions or limits on what human activities can be brought within markets. Examples include activities that are regarded as intrinsically immoral and declared illegal (slavery, child pornography), and stipulations on what contingencies can and cannot be insured, or at least require restriction to those with a direct interest at stake, such as life insurance. Concerns about the dangers of financial speculation persist, and have not been washed away by the high tide of global financial globalization between the 1980s and the early twenty-first century. They have re-emerged very forcefully during the GFC.

One of the preconditions for the emergence of markets is political and/or cultural willingness to allow market autonomy in the allocation of resources. This is a vexed issue for finance in view of its periodic involvement in banking crises over the past 200 years, as well as its involvement in more general crises such as the Great Depression that began in 1929, or the recent GFC, where banking crisis has become entwined with sovereign debt crises. At moments such as this, the legitimacy of market 'freedom' constructed during economic upswings when all seems to be going well comes back into question, and tougher regulation comes back onto the political agenda. There are, in other words, phases of tighter and phases of lighter levels of regulation. Further insights into the historical emergence of global finance are provided in the chapter that follows.

There are some additional preconditions for markets in general as well as finance markets in particular. The first of these involves stable property rights in economic assets, without which finance and capital markets could not work. The rule of law, as well as the substance of property law, is a crucial underpinning for markets, often taken for granted until things go wrong. A second rather different precondition is that of trust. Market participants, whether lenders or borrowers, or traders that are parties to a transaction, must feel a certain trust that others with whom they are dealing will repay loans, manage deposits prudentially, or honour informal agreements in fast-moving markets where not every transaction is written down. Trust is especially important to financial markets where risk is an intrinsic feature of most transactions. Markets, of course, attempt to price in risks so that more risky activities reap a higher reward than safer ones, as in the equity premium that typically sees returns from shares exceed those from bonds. Markets also permit risks to be insured. Even so, none of these normal market processes would get off the ground in the first place if trust among participants was absent and political or regulatory authorities were unconvinced that finance markets could be orderly and reliable sources of credit.

External intervention also occurs, as in the GFC, where markets show they have failed to correctly price risk, risk insurance has become almost impossible, and trust in certain areas of finance has been suspended pending improved regulatory structures. This reminds us that finance markets do not have a convincing long-term record of operating spontaneously. Crises, as Reinhart and Rogoff show in their important study *This Time is Different* (2009), have been endemic over the last 200 years. Regulation, much of it prompted by crisis, has been an organic part of global finance rather than an unwarranted external intrusion into matters best left to markets alone to resolve.

In the years immediately after the Second World War, tighter forms of economic regulation were in vogue. The twin aims here were to avoid a repeat of the Great Depression and financial crisis while creating an orderly system of world finance and trade promoted by Bretton Woods institutions such as the International Monetary Fund and World Bank. Not only were exchange rates between countries fixed, but also many individual nations imposed controls on the mobility of capital. By the 1970s aspects of this regulatory structure were on the wane, with the expansion of global trade and the US decision in 1971 to end the convertibility of the dollar into gold. Effectively, exchange rates could now be flexible. Meanwhile capital mobility was encouraged by the growing economic strength of oil-producing countries, with Western banks actively involved in the recycling of petro-dollars derived from oil-producers balance of payments surpluses into wider circuits of investment and credit. Capital controls elsewhere were also coming down as economic buoyancy increased.

These political developments represent specific preconditions for the subsequent expansion of global finance over the last thirty years. They often go under the heading of de-regulation. This label is widely used, and has a rough and ready general validity, wherever controls are being abandoned or radically loosened. The meaning of de-regulation depends nonetheless on what is meant by regulation and this is where problems and confusions enter the picture. Regulation is a profoundly misleading term in economic discourse because it confuses and conflates regulation in general with strong forms of regulation in particular. When finance is said to have been de-regulated, the confusion arises because this might mean two very different things. It might mean no regulation at all, or it might mean lighter forms of regulation that are still required for finance to operate. In the rhetoric of the idea of 'free' markets, there is a strong ideological appeal in suggesting that all regulation should disappear, and that de-regulation means no regulation. This reasoning, however, naively accepts normative considerations about the association of markets with freedom, bypassing the analytical question of what kinds of regulation apply, and why regulation occurs at all.

It is preferable then to distinguish two senses in which the terms 'regulation' and 'de-regulation' may be used. In the first sense, regulation is equated with strong forms of external control including prohibition and radical restriction. The second sees regulation as always present, but in forms that vary in intensity delivered by different kinds of organization and embodied in a variety of rules and practices. Markets are never deregulated in this second wider sense, in the sense that there are always rules and preconditions for their effective operation. De-regulation in this second sense does not mean an absolute abandonment of regulation; rather, it means lighter forms of control, which may be delivered by private as much as public bodies. Regulation in both senses remains an integral part of the story of global finance. This is consistent with John Braithwaite's argument that contemporary capitalism takes the form of regulatory capitalism rather than laissez-faire. The discussion of regulation will be continued in more depth later in this chapter.

## The major functions of global finance

The centre point of financial systems is credit. Financial institutions raise capital from investors and distribute it to borrowers – whether businesses or households or governments – who lack resources.

Without credit, business would be limited to internally generated funds and its scope for expansion would be severely restricted. This is especially true of cross-border activities, which may require costly investment to build and equip manufacturing plants, or develop mines and plantations. Corporations typically combine retained profits, shareholder equity and bonds to finance their operations. They must also have recourse to foreign exchange markets to facilitate cross-border activities such as trade and investment.

Financial institutions, in addition, use credit to boost the funds they already hold as deposits and shareholder equity. Credit helps to fund investment in further financial assets and to make loans to other credit-seekers. This often involves the use of short-term credit to facilitate longer-term lending.

Meanwhile, few households would be able to afford a house or consumer durable purchases without credit. In this sphere, credit provides an engine for the achievement of the cultural objectives that help to define personal identity and establish social status. Financial institutions play on these cultural themes in advertising, especially in retail credit and housing finance. The financial sector is therefore very far from being culture free.

Nation-states, without access to credit, would go bankrupt. All nation-states have national debts, whose scale goes well beyond tax revenue. States therefore issue interest-bearing bonds to lenders to help make up the deficit. Without this kind of credit, states would be unable to fight wars or defend themselves, but would equally be unable to fund infrastructural and social expenditure.

Without credit, economic growth and welfare would be markedly reduced. All this applies whether we are looking at individual nations or at a global economy where flows of credit move across borders. From this perspective, credit and finance are vital parts of the 'real' economy rather than processes that are somehow secondary. Food production and manufacture matter, but without credit and finance they would be hamstrung. The populist distinction between a 'real' economy that makes things and a financial sector that merely speculates with money, misconceives the complexity of contemporary market economies, where financial services are integral to global economic activity of all kinds. The dubious distinction between the real economy and finance has, however, entered mainstream parlance through institutions such as the Bank for International Settlements, which acts as the global banker for each nation's central bank.

### What then are the main activities that go under the label of finance?

It is important to emphasize that finance in general and global finance in particular serve multiple functions. A useful way of understanding this, following the analysis of Adair Turner, head of the UK Financial Services Authority, is to think in terms of four major functions (see Box 2.1). *The first of these* is the provision of *payment services,* both retail and wholesale, where clients transfer funds through financial institutions, so as to settle transactions, whether through cash, cheques, direct debit, credit cards, or some other instrument. In the case of corporate customers, this involves treasury services, where banks manage large accounts which may straddle different countries. In cross-border transactions this often includes foreign exchange functions.

---

## BOX 2.1 FOUR FUNCTIONS OF FINANCE

1. Payment Services.
2. Pure Insurance Services.
3. Futures Services.
4. Credit Services through financial intermediation between investors and borrowers.

---

The *second function of finance* is the provision of *insurance services,* including life and general commercial insurance, which represent a major strategy for risk management by both corporations and individuals. The pooling of risks organized by financial intermediaries makes insurance possible. Life insurance markets and institutions are also of massive importance in global finance, linked as they are with the organization of private retirement pensions.

The *third function* involves the creation of *futures markets* whereby organizations and individuals can pursue forward-looking courses of action in a way that avoids or rewards risk-taking. Futures markets enable businesses in particular to hedge risks posed by future changes in the prices of raw materials, or in foreign exchange rates between currencies. Airlines hedge the price of oil, by paying a small premium to secure future oil supply at a known price. Meanwhile businesses trading across borders hedge the price of foreign exchange they may require by paying a given premium to secure future delivery at a definite price. And beyond all this, futures may simply be traded by any market participants, whether or not they have an interest in the future delivery of oil or US dollars, in order to make profits.

Futures markets also represent one example of a broader type of financial instrument, namely, a *derivative*. Derivatives are financial products whose value is derived from the value of another asset (such as a currency, commodity, or a share index such as the Dow Jones) projected from the present into the future. As indicated in Box 2.2, they may take the form of forwards, futures, options, and swaps.

---

### BOX 2.2 FOUR TYPES OF DERIVATIVES

1. Forwards – contracts involving buying and selling assets at a set price at a given date in the future.
2. Futures – forwards that are traded on an organized exchange.
3. Options – rights (but not obligations) to buy or sell assets up to a given future date.
4. Swaps – contract to exchange two income streams.

---

Derivatives may be bought and sold either through organized markets or through so-called over the counter (OTC) trades between institutions and their clients. They make up a huge global market, with the notional value of outstanding contract worth well in excess of $800 trillion around the time of the GFC. They are significant not merely for the future planning functions of finance, or for trading profits, but also in the flexible supply of credit. But they are equally to be seen as problematic in that their rapidly evolving expansion in the first decade of the twenty-first century was largely unregulated, and hard to chart with precision.

The *fourth function*, the most central, involves the provision of credit through what is known as *financial intermediation*. This refers to those inter-mediary institutions such as banks that stand between investors and savers, lenders and borrowers. Their mediating roles include the allocation of capital within the global economy, and the optimization of incomes of investors, as well as the funding of government budget deficits. This function is essentially about the provision of *credit*. While banks are a source of credit, they are by no means the only source. Other sources include bonds issued by corporations and by governments, whereby issuers receive finance in return for a guaranteed interest rate over a period of time until maturity when the face value of the bond is returned to the investor. Bonds are generally regarded as safer than shares and are typically used by pension funds as a place to secure the assets on which retirement incomes are based.

Bonds, however, may be bought and sold, so the original investor may no longer hold onto them. The price of bonds fluctuates in bond markets, according to factors such as expectations about future levels of inflation, and the financial health of the bond-issuer. Increases in perceived levels of risk associated with the corporation or government issuer of the bond lower bond prices and increase the returns (or yields) investors demand for holding higher-risk assets.

Much credit is, however, organized through banks. At a retail level, they take in deposits and issue loans. But they do far more than this, especially at a corporate or wholesale level. Financial intermediation is not simply a matter of linking specific investors with particular borrowers in a direct manner, but is often a more indirect process. Here funds of various kinds, including those raised from outside an institution's country of domicile, are pooled and packaged in various ways to multiple users at home and abroad through products publicly available through the market. Banks and other fund managers offer such services. This indirect financial intermediation has grown massively in importance in recent decades during the upswing of the global economy and sustained levels of economic growth. It is, however, precisely within processes of intermediation that the GFC originated.

Financial intermediation involves non-matching or indirect relationships between investors and borrowers, who differ in their objectives and preferences. Some investors want quick returns, others operate in a more long-term fashion; some can tolerate high risks, while others are risk averse. Similarly, borrowers may be differentiated by the time-frame and purposes of loans, together with the collateral they can offer to meet liabilities. Standing between the two are financial institutions, which play a very active role in creating and maintaining markets. Above all, they are able to pool the resources of investors and the needs and preferences of borrowers to create a range of financial products that seek to satisfy the non-matching nature of participants' requirements.

Two major problems are typically associated with financial inter-mediation. One is that lenders to banks normally provide funds of shorter duration than the funds required by borrowers. Banks typically use such funds from short-term depositors to provide credit to long-term borrowers, such as those required for mortgages on property. Banks' capital reserves and shareholder equity are meant to provide a buffer between the differing time-frames of lenders and borrowers to meet imbalances and instabilities. This, however, only works if banks have sufficient reserves and if depositors and share-holders trust banks. Historically, banking crises have often arisen when these preconditions were not met, and this reflects an important sociological observation that markets do not spon-taneously generate effective self-regulation, nor do they necessarily engender public confidence. This important feature of finance is obscured in upswings when all seems to be going well, but becomes more explicit during downswings and crises.

## The recent development of global finance

In the lead-up to the GFC, it is important to understand three specific features of recent global financial development (see Box 2.3)

---

### BOX 2.3 THREE KEY FEATURES OF CONTEMPORARY FINANCE

1. Securitization.
2. Investment Banking.
3. Arbitrage.

---

### *Securitization*

In the last three decades, financial intermediation of this kind was further developed through a device known as *securitization*. Tradable credit securities in the forms of bonds have been around a long time. Businesses and governments, as noted above, issue bonds to borrowers, with a fixed interest rate and for a fixed duration. While sales are often organized by banks, these products do not appear on a bank's balance sheet. What is new about the recent wave of securitization is that a new class of credit security was created. These are often referred to as 'collateralized debt obligations' or CDOs. These may be simply defined as a tradable structured security backed by a pool of fixed interest assets, whether mortgages, bonds, or other kinds of loans. Unlike the older bonds, this new product involved the pooling of credit risks associated with the multiplicity of assets involved.

Many CDOs were based on residential mortgages. This involved the amalgamation of large numbers of loans made by banks to existing customers bundled into a *tranche*, portions of which were then sold on to sets of investors. Investors then held a more or less valuable asset or *security* which could be further traded, but had a risk element if mortgage holders defaulted on their payments. Banks meanwhile received a steady flow of funds from the purchasers of the tranche of assets. But the underlying loans as such no longer appeared on their balance sheets. This gave the appearance that banks would no longer be affected if securitized assets deteriorated in value.

These arrangements had the virtue of pooling together many small credit risks, thereby supplying a wider range of investment products to investors. The new mortgage-backed securities exhibited different patterns of risk depending on the value of the assets bundled into each tranche, and the risk of default in terms of the creditworthiness of mortgage holders. Much investment of this kind again took place across borders.

Up until the crisis, securitization had been viewed favourably, because it was seen as creating a more 'complete' market, offering a wider range of products to investors, and thus making markets better able to satisfy a diverse rank of investors preferences regarding the duration, risk-profile, and returns on investment. Securitization meant greater flexibility and diversity and seemed to be a successful financial innovation. Accordingly, it became a major activity in investment banking growing rapidly in scale from the 1990s onwards.

## Investment banking and credit supply

*Commercial banking* brings together investors and borrowers and makes a profitable business by setting higher interest rates for loans to borrowers than the interest rates it pays itself for credit from depositors and other lenders. *Investment banking*, by contrast, is involved in on-market transactions including direct investment in securities, bonds, and other financial instruments, as well as corporate advisory services, and the underwriting of share and bond issues. It has been centred, in the last twenty years, on institutions such as Goldman Sachs, Lehman Brothers, and Barclays Bank. Investment and commercial banking also became combined in the one financial institution, something originally banned in the USA after the Wall Street crash, but largely restored by the late 1990s.

Investment banking, while potentially more profitable than commercial banking, is also far more risky. This is why the combination of the two in one institution remains controversial. Investment, however, was an activity that bankers embraced with relish during the decade prior to the GFC. It was linked both with securitization and with a specific type of financial product noted above, namely, derivatives. Investment banks took the lead in marketing these products, linking in with financial institutions known as hedge funds. Hedge funds pool together the funds of large investors, including very wealthy individuals, university endowment funds, and other investment funds held by mutual or pension funds. Investment banks either operated their own hedge funds, such as JP Morgan Chase, or invested in other independent hedge funds. The profile of hedge funds within global finance has increased in the last decade as a result of the huge sums invested in them, the large profits they have made using sophisticated forms of market modelling, and the influence that they are believed to wield on the prices of shares.

Investment banking then stood at the base of a pyramid of rapid global financial expansion leading up to the GFC. In this environment, appreciating and increasingly securitized financial assets were used a basis for further borrowing and further investment, creating what is termed a highly level of 'leverage' based on high ratios of borrowing to levels of assets.

## Arbitrage

Highly 'leveraged' funds were then applied by investment banks to forms of financial trading called *arbitrage*, using highly mathematical formulae developed by economists of finance. Arbitrage in its classic form involved exploiting price differences in a particular asset between different market locations. If gold was priced higher in market 'a' than market 'b', arbitrageurs would buy in market 'b' and sell in market 'a'. In its more recent form, arbitrage focuses on price fluctuations between two linked assets, such as the current price of a physical commodity as against the price of futures in that commodity for delivery in three months time, or the price of a share in oil company 'a' as against oil company 'b'. Information on the variables affecting these relative prices are assembled and trading formulae used to identify often tiny unexplained price differences that may justify investing in one or the other security. Arbitrage trades on a large scale can make huge profits even though the profit on each underlying asset unit may be small. They rely not only on mathematical formulae but also on automatic trading programmes that seek to beat the market by small fractions of a second to make profits.

Opportunities for arbitrage are both practical and intellectual in their significance for finance markets. In a practical sense, they lie at the heart of lucrative but highly risky trading strategies by investment banks and hedge funds. Intellectually, the existence of arbitrage is regarded by ideological supporters of markets as a sign of their efficiency. This is because arbitrage is highly sensitive to price variation and the pricing of risk. It is therefore able, so it is claimed, to finding the correct price of securities, since all available information is built into its formulae and constantly reassessed nano-second by nano-second. This 'market efficiency' assumption gathered momentum in the last quarter of the twentieth century, but has been fundamentally undermined by the GFC, in the sense that arbitrage fuelled by securitized credit evidently failed to establish the true contours of market risk.

The use of securitized credit to provide the basis for investment bank trading only worked while the underlying value of assets such as real estate and the creditworthiness of mortgage or debt holders were secure and satisfactory, and insofar as investors understood the risk profile of the assets on which their investment is based. It also depended on effective regulation of the capital adequacy underlying the system, and on an effective pricing of the high-risk assets that financial institutions were increasingly implicated in. Once again trust and regulation matter if markets are to function properly. However, if real-estate values fell, or if excessive loans were made to mortgagees more likely to default (i.e. sub-prime mortgages), or if investment tranches were too complex and insufficiently transparent for investors to understand, or if the system was inadequately regulated – or if all these problems arose – then securitization was bound to unravel. This is precisely what did happen in the recent GFC starting in the USA with defaults on sub-prime mortgages and falls in house prices.

This analysis is confirmed by the fact that Lehman Brothers, the largest financial bankruptcy in history up until 2008, was more exposed to sub-prime mortgages and mortgage-backed securities than any other US investment bank. It also had a colossal leverage rate, meaning that the ratio of its overall lending to shareholders capital at the height of the crisis was in excess of 30 to 1.

Other features of financial intermediation may contribute to the instability and risks involved with securitization. One is a situation where financial institutions hold assets that are increasingly long term (such as mortgages or interest flows based on securitized mortgages) but have liabilities that are short term (such as deposits or short-term loans from other financial institutions). This arrangement works well providing depositors are happy to leave their deposits where they are, and providing short-term commercial funding remains available at reasonable interest rates to meet shortfalls in funds. However, if economic uncertainty increases, and providers of short-term finance increase the returns they require on loans, this makes it harder for the system to function. In such circumstances, the most vulnerable institutions, such as the Northern Rock building society in the UK, were those more reliant on short-term commercial funding rather than deposits. As the sub-prime mortgage crisis deepened and short-term interest rates increased, Northern Rock had insufficient capital to sustain its operations, and uncertainties led to depositors removing funds, which worsened an already bad situation. Long-term assets were now no use in the face of short-term outflows, and the society collapsed, leading to government take-over.

It is an adage in the financial world that risks migrate to the least well-regulated activities. Such poorly regulated activities included the capital adequacy underlying banking, the creditworthiness of mortgagees, the structure of securitized products, and associated derivative markets. Market players believed that they could effectively identify and price risk. The reasoning here was that competitive markets would in general discipline economic behaviour by penalizing those who acted irrationally or without taking note of all available information. Yet none of these assumptions was necessarily true. Markets do have to be regulated effectively to function, hence the need for a wider framework of analysis than that provided by economics alone, a point to be elaborated more theoretically in Chapter 4.

## Internal transactions between financial institutions

Global finance, as we have seen, performs a range of economic functions, involving a wide range of markets for basic banking transactions, credit, insurance, and foreign exchange. These activities involve relationships between financial institutions and the non-financial sector comprising households, non-financial corporations, and (as we shall analyse later in the chapter) government. But, in addition, much of global finance involves relationships between financial institutions of different kinds. Understanding such relations is crucial for any understanding of global finance and of the reasons for the periodic financial crises.

A preliminary listing of financial institutions includes banks, insurance companies, hedge funds, housing finance companies, financial ratings agencies, and a host of financial advisory and consulting firms. These bodies operate via a further set of institutions including stock exchanges, commodities trading, bond trading, and foreign exchange dealing systems, as well as informally through a host of interpersonal networks. Networks permeate organizations, and have the advantage of building trust as well as flexibility between market players, as compared with formal bureaucracies which are often slower to act and more cumbersome in their operations. Networks can exchange information quickly and effectively. They are also utilized in the illegal side of global finance, which is often neglected, but which is involved in areas such as tax evasion, money-laundering, and the financing of illegal activities such as drug trading.

Beyond these institutions are the regulatory organizations that seek to provide coherence, stability, and sustainability within the financial sector. Braithwaite (2008) is his work on 'regulatory capitalism' argues that markets are typically regulated rather than anarchic, but that forms of regulation are private as much as public. Rather than focus exclusively on regulation as a public intervention into market economies, he argues that private regulation has recently increased in importance. One major example within global finance is the ratings agencies which provide an evaluation of the creditworthiness of both corporations and government debt. Agencies such as Standard and Poors and Moody's strongly influence what rates of interest new issuers of bonds must pay through a ratings hierarchy from AAA (the highest) to Junk Bond (the lowest) status. Their role has come to the fore in public debate, within the recent fiscal crises affecting Greece and Italy. Other examples of private regulation include forms of private law in areas such as dispute-resolution, as well as industry self-regulation whether through industry associations, or through the actions of the larger and more powerful players. Internal transactions within the financial sector may then take a diversity of forms, including both trading and regulatory activities. Of course, public regulation is of very great significance too, especially where self-regulation is non-existent or prone to failure. Interactions between public regulation and global finance will be discussed more fully below.

One of the most important aspects of internal transactions within global finance concerns the fourth function of finance, as listed above, namely, credit. Here banks and other financial institutions lend to and borrow from each other. This is partly a matter of short-term or 'repo' finance, required on a daily basis to balance books. Huge sums are often lent or borrowed overnight as banks with temporary surpluses lend them to banks with temporary deficits. In addition, financial institutions may invest in each other whether through purchase of corporate bonds or shares. This typically takes place across borders, since banks in a single country are generally unable to source capital needs domestically, and because banks may see more profitable investments overseas. These elements in the globalization of finance may raise difficult challenges for domestic banking systems, where national sovereignty is seen as compromised. Overseas investment in banking has often been seen as potentially dangerous to the integrity and domestic priorities of a nation's banks, leading to restrictions on the levels of foreign investment that are allowed.

A second important aspect of internal transactions within the financial sector is the relationship between credit (the fourth function) and insurance (the second). Global finance is a risky business. Very large sums are lent and borrowed, much of which takes place across borders, involving countries with different business cultures and legal systems. The recent development of global finance has seen a greater concern with explicit forms of risk management, and one area through which this has been pursued is insurance. Business insurance has been around for a long time, and has been a particular feature of cross-border trade and finance. In normal circumstances, credit and insurance are a mutually reinforcing element in the global economy.

With the recent expansion of global finance through highly complex and highly geared forms of credit, however, insurance also expanded to cover the risk of default by holders of mortgages (including sub-prime mortgages), the risk of default by collateralized debt obligations on payments to banks, and the risk of default by financial institutions on loans made to each other. Insurance against default was offered through new products such as credit default swaps. These are insurance policies that allow the holder to insure against the risk of default, but since they are tradable, they can be bought to speculate on the likelihood of default by those not directly involved in the underlying financial arrangement. They are, in other words, a derivative. Trade in such exotic-sounding financial products tied the insurance sector to the credit sector. The health of the credit system is necessary for the health of the insurance system.

In circumstances where defaults of various kinds increase, then the entire system is threatened unless insurers can meet the cost of defaults. In the global financial crisis, the increase in US sub-prime mortgage defaults and falls in house prices from 2007 onwards had multiple de-stabilizing effects. First, increased numbers of household borrowers lost their homes. Second, this reduced the flows of incomes to the holders of their mortgages at a time when the underlying capital value of housing was also falling. Securitized credit arrangements organized through collateralized debt obligations now lost their value to those such as hedge funds who invested in them, while flows of income to banks from CDOs were also reduced. Third, all forms of credit based on the underlying value of housing assets were now compromised, meaning that the institutions involved had far less valuable assets than before, while their liabilities were likely to have increased. Fourth, credit insurance rates had meanwhile increased with the growth in defaults. Fifth, insurance companies, such as AIG of the USA, were now faced with massive losses due to increases in pay-outs as a result of defaults on mortgages, defaults by CDOs, and pay-outs on credit default swaps.

Underlying this failure, as we have seen, was a broader financial system which had fundamentally mis-priced the risks inherent in a highly leveraged system based increasingly on assets of dubious value. This in turn reflected poor regulation of the newly evolving markets in derivatives such as CDOs. The mis-pricing of risk, therefore, not only had disastrous effects for corporations, investors and lenders, but also for underlying confidence in global finance. Furthermore it was also significant from a sociological viewpoint, because it challenged the prevailing assumption amongst economists of finance that mature capital markets are always efficient. This presumption was based on the idea that mature markets typically take into account price-sensitive information. Any investor who does not take such information into account loses money, so the incentives to get it right are very large. In the event, the GFC demonstrated that capital markets are not always efficient, that risk can be mis-priced. We shall return to this point later in the book, but for the moment observe with Joseph Schumpeter, the maverick early twentieth-century economist, that markets seem to be characterized by phases of creative destruction. Innovations of various kinds do lead to genuine and creative upswings in economic development, but they simultaneously prepare the ground for periodic crisis and destruction of economic value.

## Government debt and global finance

Financial intermediation, whether by banks, stock exchanges, or markets in commodities, not only assists in the allocation of capital within the global economy, but also involves the marketing of government debt. Modern states depend on the sale of government bonds in order to finance public expenditure beyond that financed through taxation or some other source of government revenue. Debt levels have moreover been rising steadily, creating much of the pressure behind the sovereign debt crisis.

The relationship between bond markets and governments is two-way in that government activities affect market processes, just as bond market activities affect processes of government. National governments influence bond markets and global finance in several ways. First, governments through central banks (or, in the case of Europe, the European Central Bank) influence economic life through official interest rates. Monetary policy of this kind is used counter-cyclically as an instrument of macro-economic management, to avoid recessions (by lowering interest rates when growth is slowing down) and inflationary booms (by increasing rates when activity is growing too fast). Official interest rates thereby influence market expectations of future patterns of economic activity, including levels of stability and avoidance of excessive inflation and deflation. Official rates also become benchmarks for private commercial interest rates, whether on bank loans and mortgages, or the interest rates on bonds. If central banks lift official rates, then commercial rates typically increase too. However, commercial rates are also influenced by other factors, including the cost of raising wholesale funds at home and abroad.

In addition to official interest rates, government activity directly influences bond markets through levels of public spending, linked with budget priorities. Government bonds represent a flexible instrument whereby public spending may be increased to meet political objectives, though this of course also raises national debt and the proportion of government spending needed to service that debt. Governments typically use public spending not simply to secure legitimate policy objectives, but also to gain the approval of interest groups, and from a party political viewpoint, secure the future electoral success of governing parties.

Relations between governments and global finance are not, however, one-way. Politics does not determine all. Very far from it, as the recent fiscal crises in Europe demonstrate, bond-holders can dictate to a large degree whether or not governments can secure sufficient finance to pursue political objectives through existing levels of spending. They do this by bidding such low prices for new issues of government bonds that the effective interest rates governments must pay to maintain or increase their debts are too high ever to be repaid. Many observers regard annual bond yields in excess of 6 per cent as unsustainable, yet the peripheral states of Europe have been required to offer in excess of 10 per cent in recent times.

Many bond holders, even in more normal times, are typically sceptical of increased government spending as a proportion of the national income. They see this as encouraging financial inefficiency and indiscipline, and reducing the scope for market-based allocation of resources. The specific interests of bond-holders and governments may therefore come into conflict, reflected through bond markets. Since bond markets are so large in value, they typically set the long-term underlying interest rates, and hence cost of credit within an economy. And while such markets are increasingly global, political decisions and public spending are regarded as key elements in the integrity of sovereign nation–states. There is then an important global overlay on relations between governments and global finance, which raises very significant limits on the effective pursuit of national sovereignty. The only alternatives to bond sales available to governments are either increased domestic taxation, which is generally politically unpopular, or cuts in government spending, which is again unpopular with those whose jobs or services are affected. And even these two policies are not real alternatives, since the scale of increased taxation or spending cuts necessary to service the national debt is generally far larger than could be met at any given time from these sources.

## The regulation of global finance

Regulation is not something external to financial markets, to be discussed in a separate chapter from that dealing with the main business of markets. It is rather part of the constitution and ongoing functioning of finance. Global finance has generated a variety of regulatory procedures ranging from public prohibitions in the form of capital controls and restrictions on speculation to private forms of regulation by organizations of market players. There are many types of regulatory regimes, depending on who does the regulating and for what purposes. These include nation–states, most notably the USA, involving national central banks and nation–based regulatory bodies such as the Financial Services Agency in the UK, and international bodies such as the International Monetary Fund and Bank for International Settlements. They also include private associations, such as ratings agencies already mentioned above, and industry groups such as the International Swaps and Derivatives Association and International Bankers Association.

Regulation has had many, often interrelated purposes. These have included the development of more secure property rights in financial transactions, risk management and problems of uncertainty, prudential management of banking centred on the adequacy of capital reserves, global tax evasion, recurrent crisis and extreme events, control over public finances to avoid inflation and to counter recession, and the management of financial volatility in relation to financial and social stability.

While the detailed history of global finance will be provided in the following chapter, we note here that the contemporary state of financial regulation is very much influenced by historical processes and experience of past regulatory failures. Finance, for states, corporations and households alike, has always been marked by cycles of upswing followed by crisis and the need to rethink and restructure. We are currently in the throes of one such phase of re-thinking and attempted reform following the GFC. Stronger forms of regulation are back on the agenda after a period of so-called deregulation that accompanied the previous two decades of global financial advance. In spite of a belief that all was well and crisis might be a thing of the past, this was not to be. De-regulation, or as we prefer to say, looser and lighter forms of regulation, has clearly failed. So what was the regulatory structure on the eve of the crisis, and what went wrong?

Global financial regulation as it stood in 2008 was a complex jigsaw of elements. At a global level, the IMF took a macro-economic overview of trends in the global economy, while acting to deal with monetary crises in particular nations, and as a policy hospital for nations in difficulty. Its place in the global regulatory architecture focused on de-regulation of markets, more especially the cross-border mobility of capital. Until very recently, the argument was that capital controls undermined the efficient allocation of resources and acted as an obstacle to successful economic development, especially for developing economies. Crises associated with trade imbalances or deficits in public finance should be resolved by fiscal stringency and an opening rather than closing of markets. IMF surveillance was limited in this way to narrow economic assumptions and a neglect of cross-border processes of financial interdependence.

This optimistic de-regulatory standpoint completely failed to see the GFC coming. In its April 2007 *World Economic Outlook*, the IMF argued that global economic risks were low, and all seemed to be well. This diagnosis was very wrong and has required a radical rethink in how the world's financial watchdog should function. First, the risks attending the asset price bubble in US mortgage finance were not picked up. Second, new financial instruments and the increase in investment based on leverage and large credit extensions based on limited reserves were not picked up either. Third, critics of the IMF point to a cultural failure in the organization, where intellectual dissent was not prized and group-think inhibited frankness. Fourth, some of the tenets of IMF philosophy such as rejection of capital controls in crises have been challenged by the success of countries such as Malaysia in dealing with the Asian financial crisis in the late 1990s using capital controls.

A second global element in the regulatory arena is the Bank for International Settlements. This is the central bankers' bank. It both monitors financial trends and supports policy analysis and implementation with particular reference to the banking system. Unlike the IMF, it was very worried about the non-sustainability of financial practices on the eve of the crisis. One of the major functions of BIS is to regulate the capital adequacy of the banking system. Based in Basel, the bank has been the centre-point of the so-called Basel Capital Accords starting in 1988, revised in 2006, and recently revised again in 2010 as part of wider G20 responses to the crisis. These accords represent the first significant public regulation of global banking. They deal with questions of the adequacy of the capital reserves held by banks. Failure of effective regulation in this area meant that reserve policy of the eve of the crisis was inadequate to sustain many banks through the market collapse, though the problem may have been one of non-compliance by banks with Basel regulation, as much as the excessively light-touch nature of the regulations themselves.

At a national level, financial regulation is organized both through the central banks that operate nationally (and in the case of Euroland regionally) as well as through the BIS. It also involves a variety of national regulators of stock exchanges, the insurance sector, and areas such as pensions and superannuation. The central banks are especially important here for several reasons. First, in setting official short-term interest rates, they influence credit conditions in the economy, and can if they wish play a counter-cyclical role to smooth out the depth of recessions and the peaks of expansion. The US Federal Reserve is the most important of these given the size of the US economy and its key role in global finance. Its easy credit policies in the period leading up to 2008 did not see crisis coming; rather, the Fed presided over the sucking of more and more funds into the USA to fund an increasingly huge public debt and an asset price bubble in housing.

Central banks' influence on interest rates therefore has very wide ramifications. Control of inflation and regulating economic volatility are crucial issues, but they are clearly not sufficient to prevent crisis. Like the IMF, the central banks did not pay sufficient attention to mounting risk in the system, and this has affected small countries such as Ireland that combined asset bubbles with public deficits, as well as the USA. However, other public regulatory agencies exist in most jurisdictions such as the US Securities Exchange Commission that regulates stock exchanges, or the British Financial Services Agency that regulates across sectors. One general issue here is whether it is beneficial to unify financial regulation as the UK has done. This contrasts with the USA where a complex set of federal and state-level regulation exists, and some areas such as insurance have lacked regulation. The suggestion is that this complexity leads to lack of effectiveness in dealing with system-wide problems.

Financial regulation is often spoken of as if it were only public in form, and this seems to be a casualty of free-market rhetoric that limits the idea of regulation to external intervention by public bodies. In reality, industry associations in finance always play a role both in the establishment of the rules of market transactions and in lobbying government on issues such as taxation affecting their members. The problem with this may be that self-regulators may not have the capacity and sometimes the willingness to regulate a sector. Take the example of debt ratings agencies that issue assessments of the creditworthiness of both government bonds and corporate debt. These assessments directly influence the yields on bonds, which are lower for the highly rated and higher for so-called junk bonds. Ratings agencies, however, did not pick up some of the key elements in the financial crisis early enough, such as excessive bank lending in relation to reserves. More specifically, they were called on to assess the creditworthiness of the new CDOs that followed on from the securitization processes discussed above. Many were rated AAA at a time when only a dozen or so corporations had this top level of rating. Underlying this was a potential conflict of interest in which debt-rating agencies earn fees from precisely those interests whom they are assessing. Like many others, they may not have fully understood the complex nature of the CDOs until it was too late.

Finally, beyond the level of formal institutions are the interpersonal networks that constitute much of the global financial landscape. These are comprised by those who transact with each other, as well as those networks of influential actors who comprise an elite level of governance linking public and private sectors. These include corporate figures, senior regulators, and influential economists and observers. Key mechanisms in this world include trust. Traders and regulators need to trust each other to conduct transactions. These may lessen, as will be shown in Chapter 3, insofar as electronic trading becomes the norm, but interpersonal communication between traders, investors, depositors, borrowers, and regulators remains a significant and probably enduring part of the landscape. Trust may be lost by experience of bad faith or malfeasance, as occurs when insider trading of shares or bonds is revealed. However, beyond the level of interpersonal trust is a more impersonal trust in the system as a whole. This affects both depositors trust in the safety of bank deposits and bond-holders trust in the capacity of governments to control expenditure. If depositors loose trust, a run on the bank occurs and this is a kind of practical 'stress test' that reveals whether reserves are adequate to meet the challenge. If bond-holders lose trust, governments either find they cannot market new bond-issues and hence cannot meet debt obligations, or that they can only sell bonds by paying a very high interest rate which itself adds to future debt servicing requirements. Examples of each occurred during the financial crisis. Trust should therefore be included as a form of regulation which sets limits to the capacity of financial institutions and governments to function, while equally underwriting confidence and opportunity. Markets by themselves cannot guarantee trust, and in failing spectacularly during crises, destroy trust as well as value.

## Conclusion

This chapter explains what global finance does. It focuses on the contemporary financial world looking at the functions of finance and some recent developments leading up to the GFC. The approach is sociological rather than narrowly economic. Markets are very important and autonomous institutions but they are not free-standing and are influenced by the surrounding political and cultural environment, while equally shaping and re-shaping that environment. The chapter includes financial regulation as an issue that is internal to markets, rather than an extraneous and unwarranted limitation on economic freedom. In avoiding the rhetoric of free markets, however, it is equally important to recognize that without financial markets, economic growth and development would grind to a halt. They are part of the real economy. It is equally important then to avoid the populist anti-financial rhetoric that sees finance as mired in dark antisocial forces or at least as a secondary part of the economy that needs strong regulation. Global finance increases risk, and can destroy value, as much as it creates opportunity. To advance beyond battles of rhetoric, we look in the next chapter at the history of finance, and then in the following chapter at the people who inhabit finance.

# 3

# THE HISTORY AND SOCIAL GEOGRAPHY OF GLOBAL FINANCE

Global finance goes back a long way in time, and is by no means confined to the modern West. Like the history of globalization itself, global financial processes and institutions have evolved over centuries, even millennia. They are integral not simply to the development of global markets and economic systems, but also in the rise of effective states, and in the development of new cultures of economic expansion and transformation.

Finance presupposes the existence of money. And it is money, as Niall Ferguson points out in *The Ascent of Money* (2008) that 'crystallizes' relationships between lenders and borrowers through provision of credit. Such processes involve financiers of various kinds as an increasingly distinct and influential occupational group. Max Weber, the pioneering historical sociologist of economic life, is one of a number of observers who have drawn attention to conflicts between creditors and debtors within the history of monetized economies. The profit-seeking interests of creditors, typically organized through banks, clash with those of debtors – whether in industry, government, or households – who have wished to obtain credit on the cheapest possible terms. Bitter conflicts arise across history where the terms of credit clash in fundamental ways with the viability and autonomy of businesses, states, and families.

While finance has typically called for low inflation to protect the value of money, states, eager to pursue expensive wars or satisfy the welfare demands of populations, have tolerated inflation to achieve their objectives. And while finance is typically pro free trade and economically cosmopolitan, manufacturing industry has at many points in history been more protectionist, preferring tariff barriers to global competition. Finance has then a chequered history of involvement in conflicts over state budgets, trade policy, and the democratic politics of welfare provision.

In this chapter, a summary of these long-run developments is provided across both time and space. This reinforces the idea that financial markets cannot be understood in purely economic terms, but rather as an integral part of interactions with wider political and cultural forces. The chapter also provides a longer-term perspective on the history of financial crisis, volatility, and reorganization.

## A short historical sociology

Global finance pre-supposes money and cross-border activity involving credit. In ancient history, a range of objects from cowrie shells and rings to gold and metallic coinage served as money. The functions of money included service as a unit of account, a means of exchange, and a store of value. These functions for money can be traced back to ancient Babylon in the third millennium BC. Cross-border trade, so crucial to the development of global finance, typically linked money with credit, in the sense that returns on goods traded over distances would not be immediately available. Credit, involving the payment of interest to the provider, was necessary for long-distance trade to function on any scale. States meanwhile took over the organization and regulation of coinage largely to pay for warfare.

The more detailed narrative of global finance begins to a large extent with cross-border trade. Merchants operating in and through different trading ports and cities along cross-regional trade routes have, for several millennia, required credit to conduct their operations as well as financial devices that enabled them to organize acceptable forms of payment in multiple locations. The trade routes that linked China, Central Asia, and India in the East with the Middle East and Mediterranean, and thence onward to Northern and Western Europe, may not have been global in a comprehensive sense, but they were both trans-continental in scope, and highly mobile in form. Ideas and institutions as well as goods travelled along trade routes such as the Silk Road, the maritime linkages across the Indian Ocean, and through trading cities such as Venice.

Amongst the financial devices that arose from this context were bills of exchange, which date back to eighth-century China. These were written instruments whereby a trader (the drawer) instructed another party (the drawee) to pay a given sum to a third party (the payee) on or by a specific date. Bills of exchange were then as good as money, but in an era before bank notes and cheques, they had the further advantage of portability across great distances and borders between states in comparison with far heavier and more cumbersome gold and silver.

Bills of this kind were taken up throughout the cross-border trading networks of the medieval world, moving from China, through the Arab world, to Italy. They were in a sense the forerunners of cheques, which emerged later but which were another form of finance based on con-vertibility between paper-based instruments and precious metals. Over time, the emergence of specialist financial institutions, namely banks, took over the processing or discounting of bills of exchange, which could be passed on through a chain of traders, providing a flexible as well as portable means of payment. Regulation of such activities was generally through merchants' law, or *lex mercatoria*, a system of self-regulation that grew up among merchants themselves.

Yet the historical sociology of global finance is not simply a matter of cross-border trade. It also involves states of various kinds. The first banks emerged within the Italian city-states of the fourteenth century, spreading outward across Europe. These were involved in both commercial activity based around trade and the financing of government. Italian families such as the Bardi, Peruzzi, and Medici lent both to royal houses and to the papacy, itself a territorial state as well as a major cross-border religious entity.

States sought out credit, especially to pay for warfare, while the papacy required banking support to deal with the multiplicity of currencies in which its revenue and expenditure was denominated. Foreign exchange functions were therefore also at stake alongside credit. However, public finance drew from the outset on lenders located outside the state in question – Italian financiers of the fourteenth and fifteenth centuries supporting the English and French thrones, anticipating the subsequent development of worldwide credit markets for governments.

State or public banks also began to emerge at this time, including the first state bank of deposit in Genoa in 1407. As the economic centre of gravity of Europe swung northward, the Bank of Amsterdam emerged two centuries later as a bank of deposit and exchange, with the responsibility for the supply of a standardized currency in the United Provinces, later known as the Netherlands.

It has been the sheer expense of warfare that underlines much of the historical sociology of public finance. This has centred on another major financial device – the bond. Bonds are instruments issued by a state or corporation, whereby the purchaser of the bond is paid regular interest at a given level in return for the purchase price. For states, they provide a major source of finance alongside taxation. Public bonds were pioneered in Italy as a means of financing warfare between city-states. They were then taken up by the emergent nation-states of Europe, again largely to fund warfare. The function of the Bank of England, established in 1694, was to assist the government in funding war, gaining over time further privileges in the issue of paper bank-notes. These represented a further development of the earlier promissory notes such as bills of exchange. Bank-notes did not bear interest, but they were backed by gold reserves and could be exchanged in trade without the need to hold bank accounts.

Wars at that stage were local or regional rather than global in scope. Nonetheless the bond became a way in which states funded warfare whether through local, regional, and, finally in the twentieth century, the two world wars. Beyond this, the expansion of the nation-state over the last two centuries has added other large categories of public spending such as economic infrastructure and social or welfare state expenditure. Bonds, alongside taxes, continue to play a major role in underwriting public spending and thus the fiscal sustainability of states.

The major institutional innovation of banking has continued in parallel with that of government bonds, and is intimately connected with the role of credit in international trade, industrialization, and empire. Banks on the eve of the late eighteenth-century Industrial Revolution had expanded beyond the significant but limited innovations of Italian finance. First came the use of cheques and direct debit transactions whereby merchants could arrange for their own accounts at a bank to be debited and another's account credited. In the global trading city of Amsterdam, the Amsterdam Exchange Bank, set up in the early seventeenth century, used these instruments to assist merchants in dealing with a complex expansion of payments in multiple currencies. Second came fractional reserve banking, whereby banks lent out more than the value of reserves that they held in the form of deposits. This went beyond the Exchange Bank's strict policy of not allowing deposits to exceed reserves. Bank lending by newly established banks such as the Swedish Stockholms Banco entered credit markets, a practice extended ever since. Credit risks henceforth raised the problem of what optimal relationship should exist between loans and reserves, an issue which has become periodically salient ever since in the succession of banking crises leading up to the recent GFC.

Banks thereafter grew in scale and significance, though there are significant differences in how far they were oriented to global as distinct from local or national activities. In the UK, for example, the City of London became a key element in the economic expansion of empire in the eighteenth and nineteenth centuries, concentrating on the issue of bonds to countries and commercial ventures the world over. At its core were merchant banks with a global outreach such as the Rothschilds, Barings, Hambros, and Lazards. By the eve of the First World War, around a billion US dollars worth of foreign bonds were issued from London each year to foreign governments from China and Brazil to Denmark and Austria, as well as local municipalities such as Stockholm and Vancouver. Commercial banks, meanwhile, took in deposits and made loans, but in Britain their role in providing credit for industry was significantly less than in continental Europe.

Capital markets included both markets for bonds – corporate as well as governmental – and markets for equities. The origin of corporate bonds is somewhat later than government bonds, dating from the seventeeth century and initiatives of the Dutch East India Company in the 1620s. It became more widespread in the mid–nineteenth century as a means of financing transportation, notably railway building. In spite of episodes of default, the use of such bonds has continued to expand ever since – first in areas such as public utilities, and more recently in manufacturing and service sectors, with a major spike in corporate bond issuance in the global financial expansion from 1990 to 2008. While bonds are issued by governments and corporations, there is a strong market for secondary (i.e. subsequent) bond trading. Much of this is centred on the City of London and Chicago. The value of global bonds outstanding in 2009 stood in excess of $80 trillion. This comfortably exceeds the global value of shares, by around 60–70 per cent. This reflects the importance of bonds in the financing of states, and the widely held view that government bonds are the safest form of investment because they are extremely unlikely to default. Whether this belief will survive the current fiscal crises of several nation-states in Europe remains to be seen.

Stock exchanges are a further feature of global finance, especially where equities are traded across borders. They depend on the existence of organizations wishing to raise finance by selling shares in their capital base, and have a long history which probably dates back to ancient Rome. A key institutional precondition is the legal right of autonomous private associations to constitute themselves as free-standing economic entities, whether as *societas publicanorum* in ancient Rome, or joint-stock companies in Europe and North America from the sixteenth century. Autonomy here, as in the more general case of credit supply itself, means freedom from older tighter systems of royal or bureaucratic control and licensing. Many of the earliest companies were those in overseas trade where the optimal scale of operation involved the need for significant access to the capital that joint-stock status enabled. Formal stock exchanges emerged from this context, first in early sixteenth-century Amsterdam, then around 1700 in London and progressively extended across Europe and later the USA.

By 2010, the leading exchanges by turnover are those in New York, then Tokyo, London, Shanghai, and Hong Kong. Of these, the fastest growing is Shanghai, reflecting the recent rise of China as a growing economic power. Many of the world's leading investment banks, mutual and hedge funds, are also co-located in these centres. Stock exchanges, where shares and many derivatives are traded, also represent key elements in global finance. They provide measures both of the macro-level health of the global economy via much-quoted stock market indices and of the micro-level via the economic prospects of individual companies. Secondary derivative markets have recently grown up, as we saw in the previous chapter, both in relation to aggregate movements of a particular index and in relation to expectations about future movements of individual share prices. Proponents of de-regulated finance regard such innovations as creating more complete and thus more efficient capital markets able to cater for a wider range of investment options. Sceptics see no such connection between innovation and efficiency, pointing out how market instability and radical uncertainty render the confidence placed in de-regulation unwarranted.

Insurance services also have a long history, and it is one where challenges associated with cross-border trade are important. A leading example of the early globalization of commercial insurance is Lloyds of London. The informal origins of this body lie in Lloyds coffee-house in the 1690s, while the formal origins of Lloyds date from 1774. This institution is not merely involved in global maritime insurance but covers a wide range of risks from oil rigs or bridges to celebrity body parts and sporting events. Lloyds also operates from a number of global locations as well as the City of London.

Pure insurance may cover the life or assets of individuals and corporations. In addition, there have recently developed other types of financial insurance against the risks involved in financial transactions. These include credit default swaps (CDSs), whereby financial institutions sell insurance to each other covering the contingency of default by debtors. Such swaps may, however, be sold on to third parties not involved in the original credit transaction. These third parties make calculations on which transactions may or may not go into default, and attempt to measure such risks in relation to the profits that may be made from buying and selling CDSs. On the eve of the GFC, a complex network of swaps had been created, which proved extremely hard to untangle when defaults started to occur, and especially when Lehman Brothers, holder of many CDS contracts, collapsed.

Although other specialist financial markets in areas such as derivatives deal, as we saw in the previous chapter, with a range of new products, many also have longer-term origins. The first futures market, for example, is usually identified within the Japanese rice trade in the early eighteenth century. It was at this time that the Dojima rice market was established in Osaka. Organized futures markets, up until the 1980s, were dominated by agricultural contracts. It was this agricultural context which led to the establishment of the Chicago Board of Trade in 1848, and the Chicago Mercantile Exchange ('the Merc') in 1919 (developing from the earlier Chicago Produce Exchange dating from 1874). These were at the centre of mid-Western agricultural marketing. It is only in the last forty years that futures trading in these centres and in the City of London has become dominated by financial instruments, starting with trade in interest futures in the 1970s and later extended to stock price, stock index, and a host of other derivatives. In 2007, the Merc amalgamated with the Chicago Board of Trade.

A further evolving feature of global finance was the emergence of central banks with public policy functions. From a national viewpoint, central banks such as the Bank of England, or the Banque de France founded in 1800, were responsible, as we have seen, for promoting government bonds. They also acted to stabilize national banking systems during crises, as lenders of last resort. The USA was slowest to establish such a bank, relying instead on private bankers to issue bonds and ensure liquidity during crises. These arrangements persisted until the foundation of the Federal Reserve Bank in 1913 in the aftermath of early twentieth-century banking crises.

From a global viewpoint, meanwhile, the major function of central banks during the nineteenth century was to operate the gold standard, which underwrote world trade, and global flows of money and credit. While the long-run historical trend has been for money to shift from a physical embodiment in precious metals to a more abstract representation in accounting transfers, this does not allow for the persistence of gold as a symbolic source of intrinsic monetary value. The gold standard in global monetary transactions was founded on the convertibility of paper-based instruments into gold and the fixing of exchange rates between national currencies. The pegging of currency to one another through gold gave a degree of apparent stability to cross-border trade, as well as providing a mechanism for adjustments in trade imbalances. Countries in deficit on trade would be required to reduce money supply to reduce prices and make exports more attractive. This system depended on low inflation and on the capacity to reduce production costs (including labour costs) to make necessary adjustments. As it developed in the period between 1870 and 1914, transactions were typically made in pounds sterling, rather than gold itself. Central banks, meanwhile, held gold in their vaults as a backing both for global exchange stability and for global capital mobility together with domestic note issue and, ultimately, credit supply.

Taken overall, this system of global financial regulation was based, in the words of Braithwaite and Drahos (2000), on 'the convention-based co-operation of central bankers'. As the twentieth century proceeded, however, renewed crises saw an evolution away from this to the 'rule-based multilateral co-operation of states'.

The gold standard, like many other financial systems, seemed effective in periods of global upswing, but did not survive the combined effects of the First World War and the interwar depression. As is well known, the Bretton Woods agreement of 1944 saw leading states collaborate multi-laterally on a restoration of a new version of the gold standard, combined with new institutions designed to prevent a slide back into interwar problems. The post-1945 gold standard was to be underwritten by the USA, whose reserves included dollars and gold, while institutions such as the IMF and World Bank were to be responsible for financial stability and economic development.

While these two Bretton Woods are still in existence, the post-1945 gold standard ended in 1971, when the USA removed dollar convertibility into gold. A new post-Bretton Woods international monetary system then emerged based on floating exchange rates. This nonetheless marked a continuation of the new regulatory world of multilateral negotiation between nation-states. The new system saw fluctuating exchange rates underwritten by bank deposits in general rather than gold specifically. In bodies such as the G7, G8, and G20, governments took back significant amounts of national autonomy in deciding on monetary policy, altering the form of multilateralism from a rule-based to a consultative body where views were exchanged in a search for consensus. Central banks, meanwhile, have abandoned the older policy goal of exchange stability in favour of the liberal goals of low inflation, capital mobility, and economic stability. These have meant reliance on the setting of interest rates in order to adjust credit supply in ways that avoid both excessive inflation and recession. In the most powerful nations such as the USA, the interest rate and thus credit supply policies of the Federal Reserve are major reference points for global as much as national economic activities in finance and trade.

Globalization, in the form of cross-border trade and warfare, together with periodic crises, has been accompanied by different types of regulation over time. It is therefore too simplistic to think of regulation as a late arrival, finally resorted to when un-regulated or de-regulated markets fail. Across millennia, merchant law to regulate trading disputes and public currency regulation have existed in a variety of forms. As markets became more extensive and financial transactions and institutions more complex, new regulatory patterns were evident across capital and credit markets, banking, and foreign exchange, though these draw on public and private forms of regulation. What is less clear is whether there is a long-term trend in the form that regulation takes, such as a shift from heavier to lighter regulation, or (more plausibly) whether regulation moves in cycles of easier and tighter activity, punctuated by crisis and re-evaluation.

## Finance capital, global capitalism, and the changing social structures of modernity

It is useful at this point to draw together some of the broader sociological threads of this brief historical overview. This can be organized around the following set of themes.

1. Finance within the economic structure of globalization.
2. Finance capital, influence and power.
3. Finance, risk and crisis.

While these three themes are interrelated, we shall analyse each in turn.

## *1. Finance within the economic structure of globalization*

While cross-border finance has a long history, it is really only in the last two decades that notions of the financialization of market economies gathered pace. Such arguments are conducted in a range of intellectual frameworks. Some, drawing on mainstream economics, simply emphasize the scale and influence of finance markets within the whole economy, often discussed at a national level. Others, such as Paul Sweezy and David Harvey, influenced by historic traditions of radical political economy, speak of finance capital and financial capitalism, developing themes previously discussed by Marx, and the Austro-Marxist Rudolf Hilferding.

The early twentieth-century emphasis on finance as the dominant element in the evolution of capitalism stemmed very much from the distinctive experience of Central European industrialization. Here banks played a far more dominant role in economic development, sometimes taking equity stakes in businesses, and in countries such as Austria–Hungary, operated in concert in cartels. Hilferding in his major work *Finance Capital (Das Finanzcapital)*, published in 1910, saw the emergence of a new centralizing form of monopoly (more akin to what economists would call oligopoly) centred on financial institutions. This new organized capitalism was replacing the earlier competitive variety. This argument was a major reference point for thinkers such as Schumpeter and Lenin. It was Lenin who linked finance capital with globalization, through his analysis of the export of capital from Europe to the growing colonial world. While his economic analysis of colonization is inadequate in its handling of political and cultural dimensions of empire, the salience of capital markets and capital export to globalization remains a major theme in political economy.

For most of the twentieth century, the analysis of market economies and capitalist development did not give a leading role to finance. In the recent work of David Harvey, for example, finance helps to smooth the way for what he sees as the core processes of capitalism, namely, capital accumulation and profit-seeking. Yet this contribution to the capitalization of the global economy cannot, in his view, resolve the basic conflict at the heart of the system. This, in classic Marxist terms, involves a structural conflict between capital and labour, whereby capital accumulation extracts 'surplus value' from labour, thereby limiting demand and provoking crises. More sophisticated global finance markets involving products such as derivatives cannot resolve underlying tensions.

From a theoretical point of view, this kind of macro-level analysis has strengths and weaknesses. The strengths are in seeing economic systems as a whole, rather than as sets of individual actors maximizing utilities through the play of interests. Harvey's macro-level analysis helps to draw attention to the structures of economic life, and their connection with inequality and crisis. The weaknesses, however, lie in perpetuating the older theory of surplus value, which smuggles moral assumptions about perceived injustices of labour's role in production into the analysis of the economy. Endemic financial crises across history have alternative causes that have more to do with risk and lack of effective regulation. They also require greater insight into macro–micro interactions, including the attempt of participants to understand and act more effectively within markets in pursuit of household, corporate, and state interests.

Over the last twenty years, a renewed emphasis on the centrality of finance to the global economy has emerged in debates around 'financialization'. While this phenomenon has been defined in different ways, the major proposition underlying them is that finance has recently become a far more important part of economic life relative to manufacturing and non-financial services. This applies both to national economies such as the USA and Britain and to the global economy as a whole.

Increased financialization can be measured through increases in the share of finance within the gross domestic product (GDP) of key national economies. This shows up as part of the relative expansion of services and the relative decline in manufacturing. However, financialization is best captured through measures of where profit is generated. Within the USA, profits generated within finance trebled between 1980 and 2003 as a proportion of GDP, whereas manufacturing profits showed no net increase over the same period. The profit trajectory of finance contrasts markedly with that of other segments of the growing service sector. Thus the relative share of finance within total US corporate profits rose over the same period from around 15 per cent to 45 per cent, while the share of profits derived from non-financial services remained less than 10 per cent across the period as a whole. Similar patterns have been detected across leading OECD countries in Europe, together with Japan, South Korea, and Mexico. Similarly, while employment in services has grown relative to the economy as a whole in the years leading up to the GFC, there has been little relative increase in financial employment. Financialization is therefore a global process that is distinct from the idea of a post-industrial, service-based society.

Further indicators of the significance of financialization appear in a trend for manufacturing companies to generate an increased proportion of their profits from financial transactions, rather than sale of manufactured products. Firms such as General Electric, General Motors, and Ford created internal financial units, initially to offer financial services to support customer purchase of manufactured products. However, over time, a number of these units, notably GE Capital, diversified into wider financial services unrelated to such purchases, such as credit cards and mortgage insurance. This led to an increase in the proportion of profits within the non-financial sector derived from financial investments as opposed to traditional manufacturing. Such financial profit sources include interest income, dividends, and sales of capital assets. These reflect a tighter global competitive environment for manufacturing, especially in higher-cost North American and European producers. But they also reflect a changing view of the nature of corporations as economic actors.

Underlying statistical indicators of financialization are changes in the way in which corporations and corporate management are understood as actors within the market economy. Older views saw firms as bounded organizational entities, typically hierarchical in form, that focused on a particular industry or activity. The newer view has been to see firms as bundles of assets that can be traded to maximize income streams for shareholders. This displaces the focus from the internal functioning of the corporation to external considerations of shareholder values. Rather than being grounded in a long continuous history of corporate production, corporations now have more uncertain futures. Take-overs and the shuffling and reshuffling of assets through asset-stripping and re-structuring proceeded, success being measured by stock market performance, and engineered by financial investors, many of them organized in private equity firms.

The increased importance of stock market value within corporations is also closely linked with an increased role for financial controllers. Accounting and accounting standards, in this context, take on an even greater significance than before. Trust emerges, once again, as a particularly crucial element within global finance, since the judgements of accountants and auditors, as further assessed by ratings agencies, make little sense if accounts are not transparent and if ratings agencies fail to carry out proper diligence. The GFC raised major concerns in this area, because accountants and ratings agencies failed to give adequate warning of imminent problems likely to create radical financial instability.

These then are broader structural and cultural features of financialization. They indicate a new rather different phase in the structural development of finance capital than that analysed by Hilferding and Lenin. In the earlier phase, export of commodities linked with a fusion between finance and industrial capital – at least in central Europe – was both globally dynamic and crisis-prone. In the most recent phase, the financial sector has been even more dominant as a direct source of profit driven by the massive scale and intensity of cross-border transactions. Even industry has relied more on portfolio investment and financial services associated with its manufactures than it did before.

The emphasis on financialization discussed here represents a real trend in the structure of global capitalism, yet it is equally important to stress its limits. First, much of the extremely profitable performance of the financial sector was based on what Haldane and his colleagues call a 'risk illusion'. This refers to the failure of global finance to measure and price risk correctly. This meant that the book values of financial profits and assets were hugely inflated, as revealed in the GFC, and hence illusory. Second, the highly profitable performance of finance turns out to be a cyclical phenomenon connected with the long-wave of financial expansion from the 1990s. This was not financially sustainable, not through bad luck, but because finance failed to grasp the volatility of financial markets. A mirage was thereby presented as a miracle.

## 2. Finance capital, influence, and power

Because credit is so crucial to the viability of corporations and states, it is no surprise that bankers and financiers exert considerable power and influence in the operation and regulation of markets, and in wider political and cultural domains. Two initial examples of the power of finance are instructive.

The first is historical and dates from 1870 when Prussia defeated France in the Franco-Prussian war, leaving the French state to finance huge war debts. It was at this point that the Rothschild private banking family, operating throughout Europe, stepped in to take on the funding of the entire French national debt. This indicates the power of cross-border financial interests over the supposed sovereignty of nation-states during social and political crises. Similar situations have occurred more recently, as some of the sovereign debt crises that have arisen in the aftermath of the GFC, and national attempts to bail out banks while also cutting public expenditure. While every crisis has its own national particularities, a common theme is the presence of a powerful elite world of private and public financial institutions – whether bond-holders or global regulators such as the IMF. They operate by promoting particular policy options to political leaders and legislatures in return for public and private funding of national sovereign debts. There is a huge democracy deficit at work here, in that citizens both feel and become powerless to influence outcomes.

Severe austerity measures typically lack legitimacy, and national politicians have rarely educated public opinion in the realities of fiscal crisis and the role of bond–holders in funding deficits.

The second example of financial power is in the concentrations of effective market power that have seen the emergence of fewer larger banks, insurance companies, fund managers, and hedge funds. Such trends do not necessarily prevent the exclusion of newcomers, especially in investment banking or specialist financial services. Nor do they necessarily inhibit competition. However, the growth of giant institutions influences the structure of power in society in a number of ways. One is through the belief that some institutions are too big to fail. While the demise of Lehman Brothers in the GFC indicated that this is not always the case, this severity of this recent crisis and the complex sets of losses only slowly revealed after Lehman went down may have hardened the view that such failures should not be allowed in future. This is equivalent to saying that large private corporations have an automatic public insurance policy paid for by citizens. This policy effectively protects corporations against future collapse. Another dimension of large corporate power is through a tendency to by-pass or evade regulation. Finance capital gravitates to a large degree to areas where regulation is weakest – which in the run up to the GFC meant derivatives markets. This capacity will continue into the future albeit in new forms – such as within the so-called 'black pools' where an increasing amount of equities are being traded outside more transparent stock markets.

Power can be defined in a number of ways. Some definitions emphasize coercion. This may mean the use of force and organized violence (or at least the threat of its use), but it may equally mean the deployment of economic and cultural assets in ways that constrain and re-shape social relationships. Financial power is of the latter kind exercised both through markets, and through wider social relationships that surround them. The discursive power of the economics of finance has been a key aspect of such processes, because it enters into both the ways that markets are understood and the ways they are constructed and re-structured over time. This, however, shades into what some call 'soft power', and which sociologists refer to as legitimacy. While the playing out of the GFC has led to few changes in the structure of market power, it has created a profound 'legitimation crisis' for global finance, which at the time of writing has been hard to resolve simply through the re-affirmation of older mantras about free markets.

## 3. Finance, risk, and crisis

The history of global finance has been plagued with recurrent crises. The recent GFC is neither unusual nor unprecedented, although it does have some features that are specific to it. While many observers saw the financial upswing that started in the late twentieth century as ongoing and sustainable, this proved short sighted. Rather the current crisis of 2008–10 marks a return to a more normal pattern of upswing succeeded by crisis.

Reinhart and Rogoff in *This Time is Different* (2009) identify the specific characteristics and chronology of financial crises. Not all of these are global in scope, but most have some kind of global or at least cross-border and cross-regional significance. Four major types of financial crisis are identified, namely banking, currency, debt, and inflation. These can occur separately or in some kind of combination.

*Banking crises* have been endemic in the history of finance. They typically take the form of runs on banks, where depositors want to withdraw deposits and banks have difficulty in meeting these demands. Runs stem from the structure of financial intermediation, discussed in Chapter 2, where banks borrow short term, but lend long term. The problem is worsened by excessive borrowing in relation to reserves. Financial institutions other than banks, such as hedge funds, can also run into crisis if their activities are structured in the same way. Bank crises in the eighteenth and nineteenth centuries were often national in scope. However, wherever cross-border capital mobility is operating, it is likely that such crises involve an international dimension. This typically involves large capital inflows in the lead up to crisis, often associated with asset price bubbles. Globally significant banking crises are evident in 1825, 1873, 1890, 1907, 1914, 1929, 1931, 1987, 1995, 1997–98, and 2008–11, when at least two major world regions were affected.

*Currency crises* are also endemic through history though they typically centre on state policies rather than banking. Currency debasement, through changes in the composition of metal coinage, has been practised by political authorities from ancient times up until the nineteenth century. The more typical currency crises of the modern period are associated with mounting government debt, inflation through the printing of currency, and often debt crisis, the third major form of financial crisis. These typically result in a collapse of the value of the national currency leading to exchange rate crises. Almost all emerging economies have experienced such crises, from the USA in the late nineteenth century to Latin America in the 1980s and Asia in the 1990s. The effects of such crises are transmitted across borders through outward flows of capital and disruption to trade.

*Debt crises* involve some kind of default on debt, whether domestic or external. The recent phases of the GFC have taken the force of a sovereign debt crisis concentrate in Europe. Deliberate inflation through the printing of money is akin to a de facto rather than de jure default. Sovereign debt default is endemic across time and space, rather than being particular to a specific region (such as Latin America), or time period (such as early industrialization). External default is evident through the late medieval period into the modern history of Europe, while twentieth-century Asia and Africa have seen a number of sovereign defaults alongside Latin America. In Europe, twentieth-century defaults were concentrated in the interwar depression period.

However, debt re-structuring to avoid default is equally a major symptom of debt crisis. This is evident in contemporary Europe in Greece, Ireland, Italy and Portugal (at the time of writing). Here EU policy-makers have attempted to intervene before default crises, in parallel with a rethink by the IMF on its previous tendency to wait for a crisis to play out before intervening with financial support and policy advice.

*Inflation crises* seem from a historical point of view to be an inescapable feature of emerging economies. Most countries in Africa, Asia, and Latin America, have experienced inflation crises since 1945, and these as we have seen go hand in hand with currency crises. They are typically also linked with government policy, though debt crises themselves do not necessarily go hand in hand with inflation. In any case, inflation crises tend to create dollarization, meaning the use of dollars as a hard currency for transactions. This kind of financial globalization tends to reduce national autonomy because dollarization requires very painful cuts in public expenditure. In addition, further problems have arisen as a result of the controversial policies of the post-war IMF assistance packages demanding deregulation and spending cuts in return for financial support.

This typology is analytically useful. However, the endemic nature of various crises in particular nations, even when they spill over borders, is not a direct measure of more systemic crises in global finance. It is therefore necessary to take a broader view of the dynamics and tensions within financial globalization to determine how far systemic issues are at stake.

One way of doing this is through notions of *risk and uncertainty*. The sociology of risk has been dominated by the work of Ulrich Beck who famously argued that an earlier epoch of natural risks has been replaced by one of socially induced risks. Here the meaning of risk is a mix of the idea of hazard and uncertainty. Financial risks do not really fit this framework. They are both socially induced and have a long history. A more helpful framework suggested by the economist Frank Knight distinguishes between risk and uncertainty. Risks are those adverse contingencies that can be anticipated and planned for using calculations based on probability theory. Uncertainties are more radical in form, because they are the contingencies that cannot seemingly be anticipated, those 'extreme events' or 'Black Swans', as termed by Nassim Nicholas Taleb. This emphasis on irreducible uncertainties in finance represents the broader system-wide problem that makes finance markets inherently volatile and resistant to effective risk management. Such contingencies have always existed, and it is very hard if not impossible to predict when and how they will re-emerge. Analysis cannot therefore be taken too much further in a general form, but requires instead a more historical approach to particular crises and the processes and contingencies underlying them.

## The Great Depression and the global financial crisis

A final theme in this historical chapter involves comparisons and contrasts between the recent crisis and the last major systemic crisis – that of the Great Depression of the interwar years. How far has the past been repeated and how far are new features evident in the contemporary world?

The Great Depression was far more than a financial crisis; nonetheless, financial issues, many of them global in scope, were at the heart of the multiple crises that came to a head between 1929 and 1931. Five elements of crisis were present. The *first* of these involved indebtedness of Germany arising from the reparations payments imposed by the victorious powers at the end of the First World War. The massive over-hang of public debt this created for the third largest national economy weakened Germany's capacity to ride out a withdrawal of US capital in 1928. The short-term loans taken on to fund German public debts now proved much harder to renew, and its economy contracted, weakening the entire central and eastern European region.

Superimposed on this crisis was a *second* crisis centred on the stock market crash of 1929, begun in the USA. This arose after a vigorous rise in asset prices, creating a bubble which finally burst. More than one-third of stock values were destroyed, investment collapsed, and interest rates fell. This interacted with a *third* set of crises affecting the banking systems of the USA and Europe between 1929 and 1933. Depositors withdrew funds and hoarded cash in conditions of uncertainty. Runs on banks led in some cases to bank failure, and overall credit declined, leading to further contractions in investment and economic activity.

A *fourth* dimension to the crisis involved sovereign debt problems for a range of nations, rather than Germany alone. As economic activity plunged, government revenue collapsed. This led to cut-backs in public spending which further depressed economic activity, aggregate demand, and unemployment.

*Fifth* and last, the crises were poorly managed by the public authorities, more especially the central bankers of the post powerful economies. Having promoted a return to the gold standard system of fixed exchange rates, central bankers took a very passive role in the key phases of the multiple crises. In the USA, in particular, the Federal Reserve Bank, while not responsible for the financial bubble, nonetheless did very little to offset the worst effects of the emerging crises. In particular, it took little action to counteract the contraction of credit caused by the banking crisis, letting hundreds of banks go to the wall, thereby having a deflationary effect on the economy. This passive policy was followed even though the bank held gold reserves well in excess of its legal requirements. In Britain and Germany, by contrast, central banks were short of gold, and had far less room for manoeuvre. They were, in other words, locked into the same deflationary stance as the USA.

It is instructive to compare and contrast the crises of the Great Depression with the more recent GFC. The main features of the recent crisis reveal contrasts as well as common features with 1929–31. *First*, the GFC began with the sub-prime mortgage crisis, where a downturn in US housing prices led to mortgage defaults and a price collapse in complex financial products secured against mortgages. *Second* was a more general set of market failures to correctly price risk in relation to the growth of credit that helped sustain a major financial upswing. As in 1929, an asset price bubble had burst, and the sub-prime crisis and the contraction of liquidity it created also led to a stock market collapse.

A *third* dimension to the GFC was a far more intensified development of financial globalization than was present in 1929. While cross-border trade and capital flows were present in the earlier crisis, the scale of finance within the global economy was far less. Since 2007, the interconnections between global financial centres and finance markets have been far greater, leading to a more rapid and intense global crisis.

A *fourth* dimension to the GFC involved the system of international payments. Unlike the gold standard operating in 1929, the contemporary system adjusted trade imbalances through fluctuating exchange rates and huge flows of finance across borders. While the gold standard required a credit contraction in the USA to adjust to its perennial trade deficit, within the current financial system, the imbalance has remained intact, financed through the transfer of funds to the USA from countries with trade surpluses such as China and the oil-producers. These new characteristics of the system meant that the USA avoided a currency crisis or the need to deflate the home economy because of the availability of funds from other countries.

A *fifth* feature of the GFC was a more highly developed regulatory system than in 1929–31. This had given central bankers a greater role in monetary policy and prudential regulation of global banks than existed in the gold standard system. It also involved a wider set of regulatory bodies, a number of them originally established in the aftermath of 1929–31. Governments were now more happy to intervene in crises rather than simply to wait for markets to revive. Nonetheless, policy and regulatory failure was still evident in the recent crisis, partly because older regulatory arrangements such as the US separation of commercial and investment banking had been reversed, and partly because the climate of loose-touch regulation had inhibited tougher capital adequacy requirements limiting credit creation to sustainable levels.

*Sixth*, and as in 1929–31, a sovereign debt crisis became superimposed on crises of banking, credit, and liquidity. This initially became pronounced in Europe, notably in the peripheral economies of Greece, Ireland, and Portugal, but also affected the Euro block as a whole.

Historical analysis suggests periodic financial crises do not take an entirely standard form. Although common features may include market failure to correctly discern risk in the context of asset price bubbles, structural changes in the shape and functioning of the global economy and the regulatory architecture also matter a great deal.

## Conclusion

This chapter draws on insights from sociology and economic history to establish a broader approach to global finance than is usually found within economics. It shows how and why history and geography matter to the development of finance. Instead of the rational pursuit of self-interest and economic individualism alone, the approach demonstrates how finance markets are necessarily bound up with states, warfare, questions of risk and social legitimacy, together with inequalities in economic power. These broader considerations provide essential elements both in the history and contemporary functioning of credit and in recent processes of financialization. Structures of power matter. This is why the broader concept of capitalism remains valuable as a way of recognizing the overarching framework in which markets operate. Equally, inequalities of power between financial institutions and nation-states indicate a profound democratic deficit in the way public policy emerges.

Much more is needed, however, than a focus on power and inequality in tracing issues in the history and geography of global finance and financial crisis. In this chapter, particular attention has been given to inherent challenges in worlds of credit provision that cross boundaries, requiring new financial instruments and a stable and effective international monetary system. Risk and uncertainty abound, and processes of credit provision and insurance against default are particularly vulnerable to them. And while crisis is an over-used term, financial crises punctuate history in such an endemic manner that it is not clear that they can ever be avoided.

In the following chapter, the broader focus developed here is further extended to an examination of the cultural worlds of global finance.

# 4

# THE SOCIAL ACTORS IN GLOBAL FINANCE

## Market culture and financial knowledge

There is one key aspect to global finance that generally gets little attention, in spite of its centrality to the topic. And that centres on the people who inhabit the world of finance, their cultural dispositions, and the kinds of knowledge and assumptions that they bring to financial markets. In the light of the GFC, bankers, share dealers, and financial traders are typically seen in terms of stereotypes, as rapacious speculators bloated by multi-million bonuses. Such images are mollified only by the sober faces of ineffectual central bankers and public regulators charged with clearing up the mess, appearing on television or in parliamentary committees to explain why they failed to prevent crisis, and what can be done about it.

These stereotypes may reflect public anger, but they are inadequate in their grasp of the cultural worlds that traders and bankers inhabit. And beyond these prominent occupations lie a more elaborate and significant, yet often neglected, set of actors concerned with finance. These include hedge fund managers, bond dealers, commodity brokers, foreign exchange dealers, actuaries in life insurance, financial analysts and journalists, private sector lawyers and public regulators, economists and statisticians. They inhabit a range of financial worlds rather than a single integrated financial system. These multiple worlds include trading rooms, confidential client-centred transactions, boardroom decision-making, central bank deliberations, and regulatory engagements with financial corporations. This is a world tied together by interpersonal networks of interaction that link private and public sectors, as well as electronic trading networks which often involve automatic trading programmes.

Financial actors certainly deploy evidence-based economic and statistical analysis. But they also build in a range of experience-based judgements, gut feelings, and, in the case of traders, raw emotions such as fear, uncertainty, confidence, hope, and even euphoria. These may all be found within global finance, though they are not evenly spread among the various financial sectors and occupational communities. They do, nonetheless, have to be taken into account in any analysis of the financial world, rather than being relegated to the status of marginal, ideological or irrational intrusions into essentially rational processes. This applies, as we shall see later in the chapter, whether we are talking about public policy-making, decisions about investment strategy, credit policies, risk management or governance processes.

The cultural characteristics of global finance have not generally been of interest to economists, corporate managers, or policy-makers, nor did early generations of sociologists give much thought to such questions. This neglect arose from one of two reasons.

The first of these assumes financial markets are populated by acquisitive ego-centred economic-rationalists, relentlessly pursuing financial returns through economic self-interest. This approach fitted well with the expansion of global finance in the last quarter of the twentieth century when a more sophisticated and mathematical approach to financial markets led to a greater adoption of financial theory by financial traders. It also fitted well with an epoch of apparent on-going economic success. Periodic crises and panics brought subsidiary views about the world of finance markets into play, notably the presence of psychological traits such as greed and fear. This has generated an interest among behavioural economists in the psychology of market behaviour, including phenomena such as confidence, mimicry, and herding. Yet this tended to focus on sets of individual psychological dispositions, rather than the collective organizational features of market cultures.

The second reason for neglect of cultural dimensions to finance, more prevalent among earlier generations of sociologists, arose from an excessively structural approach to institutions considered from the top-down. Finance, as analysed by radical political economists, is seen as part of global capitalism, understood as a system founded on capital accumulation in pursuit of private economic advantage operating through markets for land, labour, and capital. Analysts influenced by Marxist political economy have observed both the dynamic and the crisis-ridden features of capitalism for 150 years or so, but have not taken much time to explore how cultures of finance operate, how and why financial innovation takes place, and how different forms of knowledge create new financial products and new risks. Social actors in finance are simply assumed to be driven by the system imperatives of the over-arching economic system.

This kind of sociological neglect has been overcome in the last two decades with the growth of economic sociology and social studies of knowledge. Economic sociology, unlike most of the earlier production-centred work by political economists, embraced first the sphere of consumption and then finance. Books such as Jocelyn Pixley's *Emotions in Financial Markets: Distrust and Uncertainty in Global Markets* (2004) and Donald McKenzie's *An Engine, Not a Camera: How Financial Models Shape Markets* (2006) have helped revolutionize the study of financial cultures. Pixley claims that financial worlds have to deal with the consequences of radical uncertainty about the future. This necessarily builds emotional anchorages around trust, reputation, and confidence into the far-from rational worlds of financial transactions and governance. McKenzie, meanwhile, deepens understandings of the discursive contribution of knowledge to economic life, focusing on the ways in which economic and financial thought has constituted new types of financial markets rather than simply observing and describing them.

While the theoretical dimensions underlying these trends will be explored further in Chapter 5, attention here is given to several key elements in the cultures of global finance, dealing first with traders and then with central bankers.

## Traders, electronic transactions, and trading rooms

Financial traders are the very visible manifestation of global finance, dealing in colossal volumes of financial instruments, and placed in positions where they can make huge profits and personal bonuses – as well as huge losses. As is well known, a single trader, Nick Leeson, a leading trader in London in the 1990s, made such huge losses that he brought down the long-established Barings Bank single-handed. But what kind of social actors are traders, and what are the most central cultural features of traders' worlds?

This question requires analysis of very recent changes in financial trading. These involve a shift away from face-to-face market transactions involving networks of traders to flows of computer-generated financial data interpreted by traders sitting at screens, communicating through text or voice. In contrast to traditional stock and bond markets based on the physical presence of traders in the one space, within open-outcry markets such as the New York Stock Exchange and the Chicago Board of Trade, many now emphasize a trend towards private trading rooms dominated by screen-based communication. For the Swiss sociologist Karen Knorr-Cettina and her associates, the continuous market flow represented on screens has become the dominant aspect of traders' work. Traders' realities are now enveloped in visual attention to fast-flowing forms of information that require both observing and trading, forms of action lacking deliberation and calculation. Conversation-based trading certainly happens, though it is often mediated through text-based communication systems, as in the massive daily volumes in excess of $4 trillion traded in the global spot market for foreign exchange. In global financial markets in general, however, much trading is organized through pre-programmed trading systems that automatically execute trades when the conditions envisaged in the programming arise.

In contrast with the almost visceral and highly competitive interpersonal engagements experienced in the so-called trading pits of commodity futures or bond dealers in the Chicago Board of Trade, the argument here is that electronic trading creates very thin levels of social contact. Accordingly, the human relationships that lie behind screen-based flows of information and trading seem minimal and perhaps post-social. Rather than the rich interpersonal interactions of open outcry networks, screen technology somehow isolates the trader from wider social contexts. For critics of financial cultures, this kind of social introversion helps explain why global finance ends up playing out socially destructive forms of market behaviour that create business bankruptcy and unemployment.

The wider impact of shifts towards electronic communication within global finance are, however, far less clear-cut than such arguments imply.

There are several reasons for this. One is that not all markets have abandoned 'open-outcry' systems in favour of electronic trading. This sets limits to theories of the post-social evolution of finance. Interpersonal interactions still matter, as do networks, in which particular traders gain and lose reputation for their capacity to make profitable deals. Reliable information remains a major feature of financial networks, and this depends to a significant degree on the personal sources associated with it.

Pixley sees this world as far more than an exercise in economic rationality geared to self-interest. Since economic futures are profoundly uncertain and hence unpredictable, rationality needs an emotional anchorage to assure financial actors that expectations about the future have some degree of reliability. This anchorage is provided by trust – a social quality beyond rational self-interest. Trust, however, is not limited to the personalized trust of networks of financial actors which some analysts see as in decline. This is because there is a heavy investment in the financial sector in what she calls impersonal trust. Although markets are full of distrust, the relations of credit and indebtedness, embodied in finance, require some sense of trust between lenders and borrowers. Promises to repay debt at some time in the future can never be guaranteed but the emotional uncertainties that this creates can be provisionally softened by trust that institutions will perform what is required of them. Such 'emotions' of trust are not, however, to be seen as irrational and embarrassing in an otherwise rational world. Rather, they are as it were adjuncts to economic rationality, addressing the future-oriented form that credit relations take, and the uncertainties built into it. The time-dimension of finance markets therefore matters a great deal to the social relations and cultural world financial actors inhabit. Instantaneous electronically mediated spot markets may indeed only be thinly social, but this model is less relevant to future-oriented markets, whether interpersonal or electronic. Here trust matters alongside rational calculation.

A second kind of criticism of the post-social theory of financial trading, which reinforces the sociological approach outlined here, is that trading rooms are more interesting social settings than is often supposed. Thus alongside and in the midst of the battery of screens are conversations between traders of different kinds, commenting on aspects of market behaviour that they encounter. This amounts to a 'space of sociability' (in the words of Buenza and Stark (2004)) organized in an open-plan format without cubicles or partitions. Physical space and physical closeness still matter.

One way of understanding the milieu of the trading room is to emphasize that traders' main task is to select and interpret which aspects of the information on the multiplicity of screens before them is significant. This kind of activity may be regarded as involving the links between persons and instruments, akin in some ways to the operation of scientists in a laboratory. Traders are generally highly educated, and trading rooms rely on a considerable degree of mathematical and economic knowledge. While screens are important, interactions in cyberspace do not get sufficiently close to the sense in which trading rooms operate more like 'interpretive communities'. These large rooms include spaces for discussion and white boards on which formulae and mathematical relationships may be presented and discussed. There is also interaction between the denizens on different trading desks, typically organized in terms of different specialist areas such as merger arbitrage, convertible bond arbitrage, derivatives, and so forth.

An additional way of thinking about traders is to consider their broader social worlds and how these may influence their thinking and performance as market players. Such issues demand a more anthropological than economistic approach. Some observers suggest that traders are like engineers, technically adept but socially inept. Others, looking at the elite of Wall Street traders in arbitrage, report a rich world of external cultural reference points in cinema, literature, and philosophy. Such traders are clearly not one-dimensional screen-focused 'nerds', at least in their private lives. And yet the impression remains of a sharp divide or differentiation between economic 'workplace' activities and wider interests. In the introverted highly competitive worlds of trading, the language of success and failure all too often lapses into a coarse vocabulary of sex and violence. Failure involves being 'shafted', 'bent over' or 'stuffed', success involves 'fucking' or 'killing' others. While success may mean bonuses, failure leads to redundancy.

Focus on financial transactions and trading rooms explains a good deal about the day-to-day worlds of traders, yet this by no means exhausts an understanding of the wide range of activities and locales within which global finance operates. The elite of traders may operate autonomously, but many trades are executed on behalf of the institution that employs traders or for other external clients. In the former case, what matters most are the proprietary investment strategies of institutions rather than the workplace milieu of traders. It is of course the case that traders may combine both roles and may seek to maximize autonomy, especially in relation to new and complex financial instruments that higher level managers and institutional clients may not understand.

Nonetheless, financial institutions contain hierarchies of authority and experience which creates priorities and limits for trading activities. Pixley cites the chief financial officer of a Swiss bank, who would meet with the bank's chief economist and head of trading each Monday morning to review proprietary trading positions in areas such as bond futures, in the light of current economic and political developments. In such circumstances within investment banks, institutional factors are clearly highly relevant in setting the parameters within which the mass of traders operate.

## Market knowledge – practical and abstract

Market knowledge clearly plays a crucial part in the culture of global financial trading and this is where formal economic and mathematical knowledge enters the picture. Rather than seeing traders as exclusively practical in orientation, a number of analysts have demonstrated the key role that highly abstract economic reasoning has played in financial markets over the last three or four decades. Economics, and more especially the economics of finance, has been an intrinsic part not simply in the analysis of markets, but also in the development and in some cases the inception of specialist financial markets of various kinds. Academia and global trading have been closely interlinked, especially in the USA.

The leading example of this kind of connection is the Black–Scholes formula as further elaborated by Merton, developed in the early 1970s as a means of understanding and predicting the price of options, a particular kind of financial derivative. This class of financial instruments gives the owner the right (but not the obligation) to buy or sell assets at a set price up to a specific date in the future. It is not necessary to own such assets or to buy them in the future, only to be interested in trading rights to buy and sell. While the general public may have very little if any knowledge of these instruments, they have come to represent a significant element in global finance and, in particular, in arbitrage trading by investment banks and hedge funds. The following paragraph attempts a summary of the basic features of the formula.

The aim of the Black–Scholes–Merton approach was to resolve the problem of how to calculate the present value of projected future income and expenditures involved in trading in a range of financial assets. Share trading clearly had intrinsic risks in dealing with future unknowns. How could these risks be avoided or minimized (or in technical parlance, hedged)? The model indicated that, under certain (heroic) assumptions, risks could be hedged by buying both shares and call options, which gave the right to buy the share. The formula, based on an understanding of the relative volatilities of shares against that of the market as a whole, also gave a precise answer to the ratio of the two assets that needed to be held to achieve effective hedging, a ratio that could be constantly adjusted. The hedged position was then seen as largely riskless.

This formula, while highly technical, was put into use in a practical way by market traders. Many went into the physical open-outcry markets of the 1970s and 1980s equipped with Black–Scholes formulae for the assets in which they were interested. Market strategists now based portfolio construction on the model to maximize returns while minimizing risks. In addition, new markets for derivatives were themselves created over the opposition that they represented mere speculation. An example is the Chicago Board Options Exchange. In this way, the economics of finance, and many of the leading economists within this field, who established private companies to supply share-data based on their analyses, entered into the development of the financial sector. Theory and practice were united, or, put more sociologically, economists were intimately involved in the inception and performance of finance markets, alongside traders, advancing extreme forms of social differentiation between finance markets and society. These arrangements, however, only had legitimacy insofar as they were able to convince others that the markets created were efficient and able to contain risk. If these two key elements were not met, the extreme social differentiation involved would, and as it happened did, start to unravel.

While the mathematization of finance has persisted as a cultural feature of markets and market analysis, it has receded in significance and plausibility with episodes of market instability and crisis. The 1987 stock market crash represented the first of these episodes, where share price fluctuations and volatility were far in advance of that predicted in financial models that assumed markets typically priced in risk in an effective manner. One of the heroic assumptions underlying the new financial economics is the efficient market thesis. This argues that markets price new information into share prices because if they did not there would be endless opportunities for highly lucrative arbitrage. This thesis assumes perfect information, which is a debatable one in the light of insider trading and differential access to information sources between large institutions and private investors, on the one hand, and small retail investors, on the other. However, the challenge of the 1987 crash for this thesis was to explain how markets fell so much without any new injection of information.

Further shocks in the late 1990s occurred with the fall of the giant hedge fund Long Term Capital Management (LTCM), with catastrophic losses for its investors and negative effects on the global financial system. These arose, at least in part, from the large number of derivatives contracts that could no longer be fulfilled and were thus 'left hanging'. LTCM was basically in the business of arbitrage, identifying very temporary price differences that could be used to make money. It also used current risk management practices that sought to identify and minimize potential losses and believed it had taken a conservative stance towards risk. When it failed, the question was why? It had significantly leveraged its market trading but not excessively so for the sector as a whole. The 1998 Russian default on its rouble–debt and a subsequent shift by investors to 'quality' investments was one major contributing problem for the market as a whole, and this helped fuel a panic withdrawal of investors' funds to such an extent that it exceeded the assumptions about worst-case outcomes on which LTCM's arbitrage operated. While its own investors' funds were locked in beyond the short term, other financial institutions' funds were not. A more sociological way of understanding the flight of funds is to say that many investment houses imitated the strategies of large players such as LTCM, and their withdrawals constituted such an extreme event that it was not catered for in the mathematical modelling used by traders. This in turn suggests the limits of purely economistic reasoning in understanding global finance, something again demonstrated in the recent GFC.

Put another way, the competitive but uncertain worlds of financial trading cannot simply be understood as exercises in calculation and rational strategies of self-interest, whether by individuals or institutions. This is not to downplay the importance of mathematical and statistical disciplines in the strategic shift to arbitrage trading. But it is to emphasize a wide-ranging set of extra-economic modes of market behaviour and performance that are not simply about individual psychological dispositions of greed and feed. Such extra-economic factors include a range of component parts. These include social or collective psychological processes such as imitation and 'herd' behaviour. But they also include ways of dealing with the uncertainties and periodic crises of the financial world, by reference to qualities such as reputation, judgement, and experience, which set quantitative methodologies of market analysis within a wider set of qualitative social judgements.

## Central bankers

Central bankers represent important social actors within global finance, located as they are within the interface between nation-states and global financial processes. While they have recently gained considerable autonomy from government, they remain a crucial element within public policies with respect to the economy. At the core of their work is the setting of official short-term interest rates to create the conditions for economic growth without either excessive inflation or recession. Alongside interest rate policy, central banks may also create liquidity in the system, when recession deepens. Finally, there are on-going supervisorial responsibilities over financial markets in most jurisdictions, whereby private sector behaviour can be influenced in varying ways, if central banks wish to do so.

Central bank policy settings are therefore crucial to market expansion of an orderly kind. Yet there are considerable tensions and dilemmas in performing this role. Some of these centre on the kind of balance to be struck between fighting inflation and allowing rapid growth to proceed unchecked. Others centre on the problem that stabilization in one area of the economy, such as prices, may create instability in others, such as employment. In the last three decades, central banks have tended to focus on inflation-fighting, leaving employment levels for governments to regulate.

These concerns are, moreover, global as much as national. Central banks are key institutions within nation-states, yet processes of economic globalization such as the growing mobility of capital and increased cross-border interdependence mean that they play an important role within global deliberations, centred on the Bank for International Settlements and the feeding through of policy advice to intergovernmental bodies such as the G8 and G20.

In the light of these considerations, it is not surprising to find that the cultural world of central bankers is rather different to that of traders. A former Swiss banker puts the contrast as follows:

> If you see a trading pit, emotional energy is expended and people are acting on gut instinct and emotion. ... When you get to a central bank ... every effort is made to suppress any of that. ... They are aloof, cloistered away.

Such characteristics of sober deliberation are linked in part to time-frames. Whereas traders may need to take decisions in split sections, central bankers can be more deliberative. The committees that debate and set interest rates typically meet on a monthly basis, and seek consensus based on analysis of evidence, past history, and, in the words of participants, 'the art of judgement'. Whereas trading floors have little or no need of market memory, central bankers draw on memory of past events and decisions extensively. They may take a number of months to ascertain whether inflationary trends are becoming potentially dangerous. They must also bear in mind the serious impact that may be made both by their decisions and by the way that they publicly express them. This applies especially to the US Federal Reserve whose policies influence bond rates, stock markets, and global confidence. This undoubtedly breeds a kind of public reticence, especially as to the dangerous potential created by future uncertainties, over issues such as the adequacy of bank deposits to meet highly leveraged loans.

However, the aloofness and relatively time-consuming procedures of central banking also raise wider criticism that these key financial actors are out of touch – albeit in a way that is different to traders. This criticism recurs even though central bank deliberation is now more transparent with the publication of the proceedings of committees that deal with the setting of interest rates. In an interesting panel discussion organized by the *American Journal of Economics and Sociology*, a group of panellists were asked to consider whether the personality of central bankers matters to the conduct of policy. One striking way of putting this is to ask whether policy would be better, 'If the leader of the central bank did card tricks and told jokes?' This question arose in part through the US experience of central bankers addressing the Banking Committee of the US Senate. Could criticism of bankers' aloofness and reticence be partly overcome if they were perceived to share more everyday personal qualities such as humour?

For Pixley, a participant in this panel, jokes might make things worse. Given the ignorance of the public as to the global operations of credit and debt markets, let alone the more esoteric world of derivatives, jokes about uncertainty might simply magnify fear. Yet the refusal to take on a greater element of financial education suggests central bankers are far more oriented to financial markets than any other audience. Fear of making mistakes may encourage a habitual reticence that at best speaks in a coded language to other professionals and at worse amounts to a kind of 'leadership from behind' through impression management.

Summing up, we may say that the worlds of traders and of central bankers are as much a cultural as a technically rational world. Analysis, statistical inference, and techniques of risk assessment matter to both, yet they are in their different ways characterized by cultural dispositions, which in many cases take the form of emotions – cool as well as hot. Culture – in terms of prevailing forms of identity, trust between market participants, and the valuation of autonomous markets as socially legitimate ways of behaving – feeds into the ways in which global traders do business. Participants watch and study each other, sometimes directly, sometimes mediated through network intelligence and gossip – not simply the decontextualized flows of numbers on the screens before them. Central bankers, meanwhile, rely on appeals to long-term experience of previous episodes of crisis, and on the intangible 'reputation' of those such as Alan Greenspan, long-time chairman of the US Federal Reserve Bank, in responding to challenges, largely because uncertainty and the indeterminacy of statistical analysis creates a need for alternative cultural supports such as 'trust'.

This cultural dimension often lies below the surface and is either taken for granted or unacknowledged by participants. Yet it remains important, as demonstrated in crises when things go wrong, when unforseen events make implicit features of finance explicit and the subject of social and political commentary, conflict, and political attention. Herd behaviour among traders is barely noticed except when the consensus position is wrong and vast sums of money are lost. Bankers' worlds are based on cooler emotions around the preservation of a reputation for riding success-fully through crises without rocking the boat. The dilemma for a democracy here is whether underlying financial processes and problems should require a greater degree of transparency from central bankers in the light of the GFC, or whether this function is better left to politicians, academics, educators, and specialist journalists.

## Global finance and the wider society

In spite of the autonomy that finance markets claim from close forms of cultural and political control, there remain many points of connection between global finance and the wider social domains of which they are part. These, however, take a particular form in an epoch of globalization, where the 'society' that finance is linked with is not simply that of indi-vidual nation-states and national finance sectors, but also of a wider array of global and regional forms of cultural connection and governance.

How then should connections between markets and society be best understood? The over-arching approach of economic sociology is to speak of the social construction of markets. At least three broad perspectives have been used to identify what 'social construction' means; namely, the political, the network and the framing approach. These are not necessarily mutually exclusive and can be combined to a degree as indicated below.

The political approach to markets is broader than government and legislation, being concerned with the deployment of power to shape the rules which govern markets. Many initiatives from within the global financial sector seek to set such rules as far as possible without external political legislation, or at least through political governance mechanisms closely linked to markets. In the important global derivatives market, for example, the International Swaps and Derivatives Association (ISDA) brings together all significant market players in a series of committees that have drawn up a master agreement to which all subscribe. Most nation-states see the issues involved as technical and regard such processes as a matter of financial expertise. Beyond this there is a more public overview of derivatives and other financial markets through the central bankers' Bank for International Settlements in Basel. This is largely concerned with issues of potential instability within the sector and in redesigning the architecture of private capital markets to prevent crises. In cycles of financial development and expansion, governments largely rely on central banks to exercise macro-prudential governance. It is only in crises that they become more centrally involved, supporting broad policy initiatives through intergovernmental bodies such as the G8 and G20. A major example is the periodic moves to tighten banks' capital reserve requirements in the series of Basel agreements.

The second approach to the social construction of markets focuses on networks, an issue already raised in the analysis of market trading and trading rooms. The value of network analysis may have been over-stated in particular markets such as the spot market for foreign exchange considered above. This is because spot markets require little of their participants other than a very brief exchange of immediate prices offered and sought out. The kind of trust involved in longer-term transactions is not really required.

Yet in other forms of trading, networks remain significant, and extend beyond actual trading to governance processes. Thus in the example of derivatives, already mentioned, the ISDA engages its members and associated professional experts in a decentralized network to influence or bend national rules to maximize the autonomy of derivatives markets. This approach meshes with the political approach insofar as networks are a means through which power circulates. The emphasis here remains on governance linking networks of bankers and traders, more than government through representative parliamentary organizations and state fiat. Market regulation across the board typically takes this form, with networks of industry associations, experts, and professional bodies linked with a wider set of international bodies such as the EU and WTO, as well as the BIS. Central banks such as the US Federal Reserve, Bank of England, and the European Central Bank are also key players here, with executive powers to set national or regional interest rates in the interest of financial stability, as well as an overview of global trends. Since the GFC, a greater awareness of the desirability of global co-ordination has intensified global regulatory networks.

The third approach to the social construction of markets has been termed a 'framing approach'. Associated with analysts such as the French sociologist Michel Callon, this represents an application of actor network theory to social studies of finance. Markets, in this perspective, are constructed through forms of understanding linked with technologies and objects. Markets are 'framed' in this cognitive sense, through the interaction of persons and objects that are free from social and moral obligations, and structured through processes of calculation (e.g. the Scholes–Black equation) and calculation machines (Bloomberg trading terminals) that identify predictable, sustainable, and legitimate sequences of prices that form the basis for trading. In terms of derivative markets, this approach refers not simply to trading rooms, but also to governance processes which legitimate particular ways of framing markets. The most notable of these are the ideas that finance markets can be scientifically demonstrated to be efficient, and thus require little external regulation. Those such as economists and leading traders seeking to create markets for new financial products represent epistemic communities around markets. They are differentiated from alternative ways of framing markets, whether as hotbeds of greed or unstable forms of speculation parasitical on the 'real' economy of producers and consumers.

Market framing of these various kinds produces debates, new forms of understanding, and changing forms of governance, in which external policy processes are significant. Even though global financial markets over the last thirty years were able for much of the time to persuade regulators and public policy-makers of the desirability of largely unregulated specialist markets for products such as derivatives, this broader climate no longer prevails, whether we look at politics, networks, and cognitive understandings of markets.

Andrew Haldane indicates how circumstances have changed in a number of senses. First, the complexity and profound interconnections of global finance have to be better understood among traders, public regulators, and government. This requires better understanding of risk, and uncertainty. Second, drawing on analogies from epidemiological understandings of the dynamics of disease, regulators need to develop ways of controlling or 'vaccinating' super-spreaders of financial risk against financial risk contagion. Third, system-wide financial architecture requires serious review in the light of its vulnerability to the complex interaction of financial claims and obligations. Global finance has hitherto assessed risk atomistically, at the level of the firm or node within a firm, rather than the system as a whole. In the crisis, official agreement to let Lehman Brothers fail, given the huge irredeemable gap between its assets and liabilities, created complicated and negative effects for trading partners that were not fully appreciated and which took months to unravel. For

Haldane, policy-makers navigated in a dense fog when they came to tackle the dynamics of the failing financial system.

## Conclusion

This chapter has covered the social processes that finance markets often take for granted. In the light of the GFC, these are now evident for all to see. In other words, the focus moves beyond exclusive reliance on the structures of global finance and financial markets to the broader but hitherto neglected theme of the cultures of finance. These are explored by examining the social actors involved, moving beyond the stereotypes about traders and bankers that abound in popular culture. This alternative focus may not suit populist appetites for stories about bankers and traders that portray them simplistically as greedy demonic figures. Yet it is necessary to go beyond stereotypes if we are to understand the micro-level interactions that constitute markets.

This world is also of little analytical interest to economists who retain a conventional focus on rationality and calculation, centred only on those processes that can be measured. The alternative cultural emphasis evident in the sociology of finance gives a broader account of the practical worlds of traders and bankers, worlds which are constituted both through new information technology and through interpersonal networks of judgement and trust. These are central to any understanding of global finance. They extend the macro-level focus on financial institutions and power discussed in Chapter 3, with a micro-level focus that brings people back into the picture. This peopling of global finance, discussed here in relation to traders and central bankers, helps explain the meanings financial actors give to their actions, moving beyond simple psychological propensities, to a broader sociology of motives, emotions, trust, and judgement.

We turn in the following chapter to a general re-statement of why a new start is required in understanding how finance works, and why this requires abandonment of the utopian expectations that surround market ideology.

# 5

# SOCIETY AND FINANCE

## An alternative theoretical approach

A fundamental revision of the way economic life is popularly understood is well overdue. While the theoretical basis for this revision has been around for many years, and grown in stature and coherence over the last twenty years, public debates around the GFC still remain wedded to older inadequate ways of thinking. The social and political trauma of the GFC does, however, create an opportunity to push this revision forward. So in this short chapter an attempt will be made to summarize and assess what a new approach could add to an understanding of global finance.

### The theoretical starting point

A key move in re-thinking finance is the choice of analytical starting point. Where theories start from, privileges some ways of thinking so fundamentally that it is very difficult to modify or re-think such theories further down the track. Theoretical habits die hard, especially when allied with cherished values. This is especially the case with values that are so deeply held that they are rarely made explicit or seriously scrutinized.

In the case of markets, the conventional starting point among economists is a set of actors invested with rationality and self-interest, and sensitive to price signals. Market processes play out in terms of patterns of supply and demand, and processes of competition between suppliers of desired commodities. The assumption is made that market players can rationally determine their interests and order their preferences. The markets that arise on this basis are seen as an efficient means of matching a range of individual preferences, using money as a sensitive measure of value and means of exchange. This picture is of course deliberately simple to identify the logic of markets. Generations of economists have complicated the simple picture, bringing in firms as organizations, problems of imperfect information, limits to rationality, and challenges posed by risk.

Where then do deeply-held values enter the picture? What kind of problems are created thereby? And how does this relate to global finance?

The value-assumptions underlying this depiction of markets are grounded in the philosophy of liberalism as applied to economic life. Taken in its broadest sense, liberalism values the freedom and autonomy of individuals as rational self-governing actors. Further, the relationships which individuals enter should protect and nurture this autonomy or freedom. Economic relationships in the marketplace should therefore be indifferent to the particular values and wants that individuals have. Markets are seen, in the words of Adam Smith, as systems of natural liberty, in that they are neutral between individual wants. Individual freedom and autonomy, and the indifference of institutions to particular wants, are the ultimate values that ideologists of free markets draw upon to criticize state intervention and heavy-handed regulation of markets. The moral struggle is reduced to two basic positions. On the one hand are the supporters of economic freedom and efficiency, individual autonomy, and a liberal world of free-standing actors. On the other, external forms of control that tend to subordinate individual freedom and efficiency to state-centred objectives that are both coercive and inefficient.

There is no doubt that liberalism, in its moral and political as well as economic forms, has been and continues to be a major social reference point in the modern world. Moral and political forms of liberalism tend to be critical of the atomistic assumptions of economic liberalism, displacing markets as an exclusively privileged mode of social life in favour of political citizenship rights, welfare-rights, and constraints on excessive market power. Liberalism has been a major force in both the struggle for the vote and the welfare state, alongside socialism. More radical criticisms of economic liberalism for its neglect of the coercive elements in market power obviously represent an enduring line of Socialist criticism, often couched in terms of theories of capitalism rather than the more neutral language of markets.

Criticisms of markets from many quarters have intensified both during the recent expansion of economic globalization and, as we have seen, during the GFC. Markets now and in the past have failed at key points to secure steady and orderly economic development with social justice, as indicated by recurrent crises discussed in the previous chapter. And finance markets involving banking and public sector debt have usually been disproportionately involved in crisis.

Why then has the liberal view of markets not been displaced as an intellectual starting point? Why, indeed, is the very idea of 'market failure' relatively unused in public discourse? And how is it that in the very midst of crisis, market ideologues reject revival strategies based on tighter market regulation and public policy intervention?

It is perhaps not surprising that market ideologues committed to markets as part of a fundamentalist world-view seek ways in which to wriggle out of the challenges posed by market failure. One response, typical during the cold war, was to argue that there are only two options for economic policy: markets or command economies on the Soviet model. Since the latter were both inefficient and coercive, they fail as an alternative, leaving markets, however problematic, in command of the ideological battlefield. The assumption that there are only two options is, however, most unsatisfactory, given the complex reality of public policy and regulatory arrangements. Leaving aside whether there is a coherent 'third way' between markets and command economies, it is preferable to see multiple choices being available in terms of different modes and levels of market regulation. In the financial sector, for example, public regulation of banking at national, regional, and/or global levels is a reality, but one in which the ground is constantly shifting between different combinations of multi-level governance. Within this sphere, regulation takes different forms in different sectors of finance, and has recently been stronger in relation to some products rather than others. Meanwhile, central banks may take somewhat different views of policy objectives, and have differing relationships with government over time. To speak in terms of stark choices between regulation or de-regulation is far too simplistic a way of dealing with the range of options possible. It is how you regulate, not whether you regulate, that lies at the heart of the issue.

Market ideologues typically bypass all of this. Markets seem not to fail. When they go wrong, it is because they are too heavily or clumsily regulated. Thus the GFC occurred not because of any problems with markets, but because bodies such as the US Federal Reserve did not do their job properly, or because regulatory environment is too complex a jigsaw of multiple jurisdictions.

This line of objection has more credibility because regulatory arrangements may and have had faults, the precise details of which are sketched in the next chapter. For current purposes though, the main difficulty with this defence is that it wriggles away once again from the question of market failure and market inefficiency, leaving de-regulated markets as the default setting for analysis and policy choice. The probability that certain regulatory processes failed does not entail the view that markets did all right after all. It speaks rather to combinations of market and regulatory failure.

Let us then re-state the direct criticism that can be made of market ideologies in relation to finance. It is that finance markets have failed repeatedly through the history of modern capitalism, reflected in banking crises, corporate failure, bankruptcy, and most recently huge bail-outs from the public sector to recapitalize corporations regarded as too big to fail. And there are theoretical reasons why this is so. These are connected to problems of risk and uncertainty that are endemic to credit, the lynchpin of finance in general, and global finance in particular. Credit is necessarily future-oriented. It requires a set of promises to repay at some future point, and acceptance of payment. This future-oriented dimension is not adequately captured in depictions of markets as a series of completed transactions at a given moment in time based on rationally discerned information.

Frank Knight, as has previously been pointed out, famously distinguished between risk and uncertainty. Risk relates to future contingencies, the probability of which may be calculated. Uncertainty deals with those that cannot. Finance markets have always been prone to both risk and uncertainty. However, recent advances in financial theory seemed to suggest that the sphere of calculable risk could be mastered, and thus be priced effectively into markets. In this way, uncertainty could be minimized and the future-oriented nature of credit, now organized on a global scale, could be controlled. This re-affirmed the idea of market actors as knowledgeable, and markets as efficient. The reasoning here is that it is in everyone's interest to find under-priced assets and buy them before others catch up and prices rise, while over-priced assets can be sold on the same logic. This practice of arbitrage, based on widely dispersed information, so it is supposed, makes markets necessarily efficient.

Market actors may deploy rational calculation and sophisticated statistical analysis, but this is no guarantee that this enables them to correctly price risk. Whereas the conventional starting point of market economics presumes that rationality applied to information-gathering combined with self-interest are adequate means of disciplining market behaviour to achieve efficient outcomes, this scenario breaks down when rational calculations are not sufficient. This could be because knowledge is not widely available, though if so this may be regarded as a market imperfection that can in principle be corrected. An alternative possibility is that there are epistemological limits to what can be known about the future, or, as put colloquially by Donald Rumsfeld, we don't know what we don't know.

A minority of economists including Keynes, and more recent thinkers such as Shackle, have been aware that uncertainty is a bigger problem than most market analysts presumed. It is, however, a recent string of financial crises culminating in the GFC that have brought home problems with innovations in financial theory that promised to control risk and minimize uncertainty. This process has been brilliantly analysed by Donald Mckenzie in *An Engine Not a Camera* (2006). He shows how financial theory appeared to have overcome a good deal of the problem of risk by a series of mathematical innovations. These treated stock price movements as random, but identified patterns in the volatility of individual stocks vis-à-vis the market as a whole. As we saw in Chapter 4, the innovative Black–Scholes–Merton equations appeared to solve the difficult problem of calculating the current value of the projected future income and expenditure flows involved in trading assets. Using the formula in its early years seemed to work. Future-oriented action seemed, at least within these technical parameters, to be risk-free.

But as we also saw in Chapter 4, the continuing incidence of financial stress – especially in the 1990s and 2000s – has rendered this apparent victory over risk dubious. An underlying problem with the approach was the underestimation of the probability of extreme events and this derived in large measure from the assumption that the distribution of such events followed the pattern of a normal distribution. In statistical theory, a normal distribution means that the probability of extreme, highly atypical events is very rare. The French mathematician Mandlebrot had already shown this was not the case for financial markets, but financial theorists were not convinced. The GFC, following on from previous events such as the collapse of the hedge fund LTCM in 1996, proved their scepticism to be ill-founded. Extreme events are not so rare after all.

What theoretical implications does all this have for an understanding of finance markets?

First, it suggests that rational calculation is not enough to prevent financial crisis and the destructive consequences that follow from it. This is partly for epistemological reasons. Epistemology involves the theory of knowledge, or put another way, how sure can we be that particular claims to knowledge are valid. The epistemological problems in finance are to do with the existence of limits to our capacity to calculate and hedge against risk. These problems were ignored during the heyday of financialization over the twenty years when the confident hubris of market players carried regulators with it, multiplying risk and undermining prudence.

Second, it suggests that financial markets are neither entirely rational nor necessarily efficient either. Just because markets may tend to factor in new information very quickly for fear of missing out on profitable opportunities does not mean that markets are necessarily efficient. Information, as we saw in the previous chapter, is limitless, and thus has to be both perceived and interpreted as relevant to transactions. It may be that potentially relevant information is known but not deemed relevant. The huge leverage ratios where institutions lent out funds up to thirty times the value of their deposits was clearly known on the eve of recent crisis but not considered a significant risk. Another indication of the weaknesses of the market efficiency argument is that crises can emerge, such as the stock market collapse of 1987, even without new information entering the market.

Rational calculation combined with self-interest is not an adequate starting point for an understanding of the dynamics of markets in general, and finance markets in particular. This point may be put more strongly than that. Such assumptions are a very weak starting point because they leave out so much. Among the omissions are first the structures of power and influence that markets generate that undermine the ideal of a system of natural liberty shared by free-standing individuals. These include structures of economic power, reflected in the capacity of financial interests to create new forms of lucrative financial markets and to lobby governments to regulate (or de-regulate) markets in ways that suit investors. Bond-holders are currently able to exercise financial power over the fate of indebted nation-states, by demanding such high interest rates from newly issued government bonds that the interest payments required come close to bankrupting state finances – unless other remedial actions such as savage expenditure cuts are made.

In an epoch of financialization, the centre of gravity of economic power involves investors in a range of financial institutions linked not simply with banks, but also hedge funds and private equity firms linked with bond markets as well as share markets, and with a host of financial derivatives. This suggests the bottom-up micro foundations of market theory are incomplete because they are inadequate to deal with top-down macro-level asymmetries of power between the finance sector, governments, and households. Finance, for example, through the bond-market, can determine medium to long-term interest rates on government debt, while households are vulnerable to global financial crises that undermine the values of savings and pensions, and increase unemployment.

In the worlds of public fiscal crises of expenditure or downward pressure on household welfare, the underlying normative ideals of market freedom based on free-standing and autonomous social actors seems out of place and irrelevant.

Beyond this, a second set of omissions surround the endemic problems of risk and uncertainty. Following the analysis of Jocelyn Pixley, finance markets build emotions and other kinds of intuitive dispositions into their operations precisely to handle the uncertainties of the future which render trust in others problematic. Calculation can only work reliably in relation to the past. It is far more difficult to apply successfully and over the medium to long term to the future. This argument is worthy of further elaboration because the role of emotions in markets is often misconceived.

Recent developments in sociological theory suggest that the place of the emotions in social and economic life has often been misconceived. A major problem here is a false dichotomy between rationality, on the one hand, and emotions on the other. Whereas rationality is seen as cold and calculating, emotions are seen as necessarily hot, passionate, and irrational.

This approach is typically linked with a second argument in which emotions are removed from any social context and regarded either as matters of innate personal psychology or 'animal spirits' – the term famously used by Keynes to depict the spontaneous rush to action characteristic of speculation.

Sociology diagnoses two major problems here. The first is that the span of emotions has a wider range than the conventional emphasis on passions implies. Hope, grief, sadness, optimism, and gut feeling may all be regarded as emotions, in that they are dispositions distinct from calculations of self-interest and abstract processes of cognition. The sharp dichotomy between rationality and emotionality tends to obscure that part of the register of feelings that is neither impulsive nor strictly calculative. It is, however, precisely within this register that many of the dispositions of financial traders and central bankers operate.

Traders, for example, tend to imitate each other, assuming that success will breed success, rather than being moved simply by statistical calculation, leading to the so-called 'herd' behaviour evident in both the periodic heady peaks and the dismal collapses that markets generate. As Pixley demonstrates, central bankers, even Alan Greenspan of the US Federal Reserve, combine analysis of evidence with hope and gut feeling. Even if many bankers reject the idea that there is an emotional element in their financial dealings, they do recognize both the problem of future uncertainty and the role of non-calculative dispositions. These were described variously in Pixley's interviews with bankers, in terms ranging from intuitive feelings linked to an 'inner voice', 'gut feeling', and 'prognostications about the future'. One of the most interesting examples draws on the German word *entschiedungsfreudig*, which may be translated as the joy in making decisions. This was used by a former bank official now providing advice to financial executives as a 'filter' for dealing with fear and uncertainty in financial transactions.

A second related area of misconception in the handling of emotions in finance surrounds the source of emotions. The conventional way of interpreting these is either as products of individual psychology or basic features of human nature. This approach neglects the social contexts in which emotions arise as means of dealing with the exigencies of life ranging from bereavement and suffering to financial uncertainty and fear of failure. Behavioural psychology has made a start in suggesting a broader framework, though it does not take the analysis far enough. Robert

Shiller, for example, in *Market Volatility* (1989) and *Irrational Exuberance* (2000), provides plentiful survey evidence of emotional feelings among investors. However, these feelings are seen as strongest among those prone to herd behaviour, swayed by the financial media. So-called 'smart' investors have a different psychology. Yet in Pixley's account, even the smartest are not immune from the social challenges of uncertainty which are endemic in future-oriented transactions based on promises. From a sociological viewpoint, variations in individual psychological propensities are therefore less significant than the social characteristics of the relationships that finance promotes and tries to reproduce.

We spoke above about a set of omissions in the typical starting point in economic analysis that focused on rational calculation and self-interest alone. Two types of omission involved first structures of power and domination in economic life, and second, problems of risk and uncertainty. A third level of omissions in conventional accounts of markets, that has been stressed throughout this study, involves the ways in which politics and culture constitute and contribute to the reproduction of markets. This occurs through security of property rights, legal regulation, public policy support for infrastructure and the training of human capital, and bail-outs to cope with market failure. These inputs may be seen as contextual to markets rather than essential to its functioning. Yet to argue in this way encourages a slippage from acknowledging the social and political preconditions for markets, back to the idealized starting point of rational self-interested actors jealous of their freedom and autonomy.

It is therefore time to replace the language of market freedom contrasted with external intervention with a new language that is more sensitive to what may be called social-economics or economic sociology. In this discourse, markets, states, and cultures interact in a complex set of ways, often articulated through public policy. To refuse this new language is to leave in place an ideologically loaded world view masquerading as powerful and relevant analysis. So why hasn't this occurred before?

The answer is a mixture of two considerations. One is the continuing normative force of the utopia of free markets. The other is scepticism that an alternative approach to economic analysis, based on a new starting point, is possible.

Utopias are widespread in social life, and show no sign of receding. They include visions of a harmonious and peaceful cosmopolitan world, an environmentally sustainable way of life, global religious community to end suffering, and the restoration of authentic national communities of like-minded citizens. Yet dystopias are also present, from endemic wars of civilizations without end, to the collapse of inner cities into violence, and the abject failure of states to guarantee security and an orderly life in the face of crime, corruption, and rampant poverty.

Market freedom, in this context, gains most of its utopian force from the presumption that self-interest is a universal human attribute, but that its operation can be civilized. Following the analysis of Adam Smith, this occurs through a combination of the spontaneous order that markets bring – the famous invisible hand – and public regulation of a market-complementing kind. It is arguable that financial markets do not and cannot approach this utopia, both because of their tremendous power and because the problem of uncertainty renders them crisis-prone and destructive. If the free market utopia persists, in spite of all evidence to its lack of accord with evidence, it must either be because other dystopia induce greater horror than that of financial crisis, or because financial utopians believe that pragmatic public authorities will always come to the rescue.

The dystopian foil that ideals of market freedom presuppose relies on some notion of coercive authoritarianism. If markets are either abolished or rigidly controlled as in command economies, then individual freedom and autonomy is undermined. But what if markets have coercive or authoritarian effects, whether in the abuse of cheap labour or reckless lending that ends in bankruptcy and loss of savings? That it seems is not enough to destroy the utopia. However, regulation to ratchet up labour standards or regulate speculation is very often portrayed as such a threat. The utopia is thus founded on arbitrary presumptions and forms of implausible rhetoric. It should be abandoned freeing economic analysis from its utopian anchorage and starting again.

This new start requires the abandonment of utopias of the two alternative free markets and perfect regulation. Each leads to unexpected failure and periodic crisis. Making a new start also means adopting options that are philosophically more sophisticated in that they recognize the intrinsic uncertainties and limits to knowledge that constitute the future-oriented uncertainties of finance markets. This alternative approach requires pragmatism rather than utopianism. It also benefits from a less economistic, more sociological approach.

## The economy and finance: a sociological and interdisciplinary approach

Finance and the economy are part of society. This seems obvious. Yet it currently makes little real sense to the way 'insiders' in financial worlds understand the industry, or to the way most policy-makers and regulators typically justify their actions. This is partly because of the scientific reputation of economics, and partly, as I have argued here, because of the moral and utopian foundations underpinning pro-market ideologies. Unless this utopian world view is cut down to size, finance markets are destined to fail repeatedly in the future, creating adverse social as much as economic consequences. The finance sector will become even less legitimate than it is now and populist pressure on governments to rein in bankers will increase the likelihood of knee-jerk policy reactions. Such pressures do not, however, mean that global finance markets should be abandoned and finance de-globalized. Rather, it means that the policy and regulatory options should try to maximize prudence in relation to risk, and bridge the growing gulf between finance and society.

Concrete policy and regulatory measures are discussed in the following chapter. I concentrate here on further dimensions to a sociological understanding of global finance.

A key element of this approach is that the study of finance needs to be re-cast in a systematic manner to take account of the interaction of social and economic processes. Law, politics, culture, and social psychology matter to the foundation of markets, to their internal operation, and to their creative performance, dynamics, and limitations. Applying a sociological approach is not simply to do with enriching a sense of market mentalities, including greed, fear, panic, imitation, gut feeling, prudence, and joy in making a good deal, alongside rational calculation – though this broader psychology is very helpful to the understanding of the complex worlds of traders and bankers. Sociology, however, can do more than this.

Building on a more complex social psychology offers ways of understanding how cultural expectations, and senses of trust and legitimacy, perform a number of functions within financial markets. Above all, they assist market actors to meet challenges associated with both the uncertainties and the future-oriented characteristics of finance. The possibility of radical uncertainty and crisis could paralyse market actors. Yet this generally does not happen. This is partly because market players have to trust each other – at least enough to complete transactions. It is also because market actors trust the calculative methods they employ. They also assume that their activities are legitimate because they meet wider expectations that increase shareholder value for financial institutions, which is a desirable end – not least because it maximizes their income and welfare, as well as that of others. In normal times, all this is taken for granted and becomes a habitual feature of financial worlds. But in crises, these underlying foundations of finance are starkly revealed. What is also revealed is a weak sense of responsibility for the failures of finance markets.

Whereas in normal times, the autonomy and differentiation of markets from the worlds of culture and politics is taken for granted, in a major crisis such as the GFC, it becomes problematized. Traders and bankers are seen as greedy and selfish, unethical, and too cut-off from public and community concerns and anxieties. Calls for their bonuses to be extinguished, their taxes to be increased, and for their priorities to be more ethical and socially responsible abound. While for economists these are so to speak 'noises off stage', for sociologists, these calls speak both to the continuing location of finance in society and to crises of the dysfunctional or pathological effects of financial freedom. The senses of dysfunction occur within nations, but they are also very much a response to the globalization of financial markets, beyond the apparent control of democratic politics which is primarily expressed at national or (in the case of Europe) regional levels. Differentiation of global finance from society, therefore, has national and global dimensions, and both of these spill over into politics, where policy and public regulatory deliberations are centred. And again in a deep crisis such as the GFC, politics intervenes, with bail outs of public money to keep institutions afloat.

The conceptual repertoire of sociology also describes problems of differentiation and integration through metaphors of embedding and disembedding. The embedding of economy in society is reflected in closer relations between markets, politics, and culture, characteristic of pre-industrial and pre-modern worlds. It is reflected in doctrines such as just prices and moral responsibilities to individuals and groups adversely affected by economic change. The disembedding of markets from society is associated with modern processes of market autonomy and doctrines of laissez-faire economics. Karl Polanyi, the Hungarian economic historian and social philosopher, author of *The Great Transformation* (1944), thought laissez-faire impossible to sustain since societies would always demand a sense of social responsibility from markets. Welfare states represent one form this could take in modern societies. Polanyi has proven a great inspiration to the development of economic sociology. Yet financialization tied to late twentieth-century globalization created, as we have seen, a new phase of laissez-faire akin to the nineteenth-century phases of market-based economic globalization that Polanyi thought of almost as a historical aberration. It seems then that modern economies have a more cyclical dynamic, with waves of market-led economic expansion followed by crisis, disembedding followed by calls to re-embed, differentiation followed by challenges of re-integration.

In a general sense, then, sociology encourages accounts of how economy, culture, and polity interact. This is built around three elements: theories of social action under conditions of uncertainty, concepts of the embedding and disembedding of the economy in society, and theories of social differentiation and re-integration. These apply both across phases of apparently normal market-operation and phases of crisis when the pathologies of social differentiation apply are clearly manifest. Equally, they embrace both the structures of financial power and financialization, discussed in Chapter 3, and the cultural worlds of traders and bankers.

Sociology offers broader insights than economics alone, but it is equally the case that global finance demands an even wider interdisciplinary focus. This embraces history and geography so as to integrate time and space within the analysis of finance markets. Without history, it would not be possible to fully gauge the repeated patterns of global financial boom and bust, nor compare and contrast the performance of policy options tried in the past. Meanwhile a greater awareness of spatial patterns indicates both how varied are the origins of financial innovations and how far global cities and global networks linked by new information technology are involved in the complex sets of nodes and links that constitute global finance. And beyond this, mathematics and statistics are necessary to an understanding of measurable features of global finance. Whereas the insights of sociology have hitherto been primarily qualitative, it is clear that finance is inseparable from quantification. Sociology can nonetheless add to the repertoire of quantifiable questions that may be asked of finance, including 'How far are financial arrangements socially legitimate?', 'What forms of market differentiation are dysfunctional to social arrangements?', and 'What properties of financial networks increase system risk?'

What is more debatable though is the meaning and reliability of conventional statistical analysis of finance markets, especially when applied to the valuation of risk and calculation of the present value of cash flows projected into the future. Here an element of epistemological caution is required, the significance of which extends far beyond philosophy to practical questions of the efficiency of markets. This suggests that the statistical orderliness of normal distributions may be inappropriate to the analysis of extreme events.

Without a sociological and even broader interdisciplinary approach to global finance it is simply not possible to understand how far finance markets are efficient, just, pathological or dysfunctional. Such considerations also feed into questions of policy reform and regulatory responses raised by the GFC, the theme of the concluding chapter.

# 6

# GLOBAL FINANCE AND PUBLIC POLICY

The global financial crisis (GFC) dramatized failures and dilemmas in the way public policy has approached global finance. Just as financial markets failed, so too did the policy and regulatory framework surrounding finance. This 'double failure' has been partly obscured by an ideological stand-off between free marketers who blame regulators, and supporters of public regulation who blame finance markets and the laissez-faire culture of bankers. In this chapter, we ask whether there are better ways for public policy to regulate global finance. Can the endemic risks and uncertainties of this sector be approached in more effective ways? And if so, what changes are required in the institutional architecture of global finance to bring them into being?

Such questions are of course complicated by the intensification of financial globalization in recent years. This has not destroyed the nation-state and national regulation as predicted by some of the earlier theorists of globalization. But it has, nonetheless, magnified the scale of cross-border flows of finance transmitted increasingly through electronic channels and through complex sets of financial instruments. This context does not spell the end of national regulation through agencies such as the US Federal Reserve or the Bank of England that set interest rates, or through national policies on the regulation of banking, or prudential regulation of the entire finance sector. But having said this, it is equally the case that financial globalization demands better co-operation between nations in bodies such as the G20 and especially the EU. And beyond this, improvements are also required in the functioning of global institutions such as the International Monetary Fund, or the Bank for International Settlements, in the way that the global financial system is monitored and supervised and crises averted or minimized in their consequences.

Such challenges of public regulation should not of course obscure problems with de-regulated markets and the inadequate self-regulation by the finance industry of sectors such as derivatives, or processes such as credit rating. In this sense, it is improvements in the relationship between market processes and players, on the one hand, and public regulation, on the other, that matters most rather than public policy reform alone.

This chapter is also informed by the broad sociological view of finance elaborated in earlier chapters. This extends the analysis beyond finance markets bringing together investors and credit-seekers of various kinds mediated through the price of credit. Finance markets embody the pursuit of rational self-interest, but they are also arenas of risk and uncertainty, of social emotions such as trust, imitation, and panic, and places where culture and politics influence and shape judgements and the operation of financial institutions. The belief that financial players should be left alone by the rest of society so they can generate economic goods and improved welfare by operating efficient money markets is a cultural belief that many dispute, including many friends of market mechanisms.

A theoretical problem with laissez-faire assumptions of this kind is that of excessive social differentiation of economy from society. This involves a mismatch between wider cultural and political expectations of the economy and the self-centred and often self-serving world of financial traders and bankers. The sub-culture of global finance appears so differentiated from society because its denizens, particularly those at the top are buffered against the uncertainties and risks of everyday life through large salaries and bonuses and an irrational belief that market processes can be fully understood through mathematical modelling. The faltering and embarrassed stance of bankers appearing recently at televised meetings of parliamentary committees under tough questioning by parliamentarians provides an important public indication of a clash of different worlds, reflected in a severe reputational crisis for the finance industry and its leaders.

We raise this wider sociological framework here to provide a broader basis for the evaluation of the various reforms that have been proposed for global finance in the light of the GFC. Public policy initiatives may be assessed in terms of a broad range of economic objectives from their contribution to financial stability and avoidance of inflation, to economic growth and increased employment. However, broader criteria matter too, including contributions to social cohesion, the cultural legitimacy of finance, and the democratic accountability of financial markets and institutions to political processes. These criteria are partly a matter of the public reputation of bankers and the legitimacy of the finance industry, but in more extreme circumstances, of the capacity of social life and governance to continue in a sustainable way. More dire crises of this kind are evident at the time of writing in many parts of Europe, where a fiscal crisis of the state has combined with the general adverse impact of the earlier banking crisis. There are never solely market-based solutions to such crises, whether organized through cuts to public expenditure to satisfy creditors – current and future – or in terms of increased taxation to help balance books. Market problems become political problems, and political problems move beyond legislative and regulatory form, when deep-seated questions of fairness and social justice become involved. Questions therefore arise as to how various recipes for reform might assist social cohesion and restore public legitimacy and confidence.

In the light of these general considerations, we now turn to public policy initiatives proposed in the light of the GFC.

## Causes of the global financial crisis

To sort out what should be done, in the light of the GFC, depends on what is taken to be the leading causes of the crisis. This is not such an easy or straightforward exercise. Howard Davies, former head of the Financial Services Authority, in his review of the GFC identifies around thirty-eight causes that have been canvassed by observers. These range from macro-economic imbalances in global trade and financial flows, through dysfunctional properties of financial markets for derivatives and regulatory failure, to broader possibilities such as an excess of testosterone in trading rooms. If trade imbalances were the key reason for crisis, then public policy responses in the field of global trade policy would be appropriate, whereas if excess testosterone were the problem, then perhaps trading rooms should operate according to a more explicit code of professional ethics designed to curb irrational exuberance and create a culture more open to women traders. Analysis does, however, have to move away from single-factor explanations and long lists of multiple causes to get very far. A more discriminating approach is to select the more important causes and consider interactions between them.

One way of doing this is to group contributory causes into three categories (see Box 6.1). These may be considered in turn.

---

**BOX 6.1 CONTRIBUTORY CAUSES OF GFC**

1. Macro-economic imbalances.
2. Market failure.
3. Policy and regulatory failure.

---

## Macro-economic imbalances

One of the fundamental underlying causes of the GFC is widely thought to be the trade imbalance between the USA, which is the leading deficit country, and China, the leading surplus country. The existence of this imbalance means that the USA, together with some other advanced European countries, run their national economies in deficit and must rely on flows of finance into deficit countries from countries of surplus, such as China, Japan, and the oil-producing nations. Such flows are forthcoming because the USA has been seen as a safe haven for finance, and because the dollar is the leading trading currency. Such funding flows into apparently safe assets create a kind of self-insurance for surplus countries held against future uncertainties. Much of this finance is used to purchase US government debt, in the form of Treasury bonds. China has accumulated well in excess of \$1 trillion of these. Global inflows of funds finance both the US trade deficit and the US government's large budget deficit.

Financial globalization in this sense keeps the US economy and government afloat. Without these financial inflows, the USA would have to increase export earnings relative to imports in a global climate of increased competition in manufacturing, and increase domestic savings, or try to resort to protectionist policies. Curtailment of imports relative to exports would also tend to limit consumer spending. Making the necessary adjustments here would be very painful economically and socially including downward pressure on employment levels, but adjustment has been inhibited by funding inflows. Even more significantly perhaps, funding inflows also underwrite two further processes: one is the government budget deficit; the other, low interest rates which in turn means cheap credit.

East Asian savings have therefore allowed the USA to postpone serious attempts to re-balance budgets, while allowing cheap credit to further boost consumption and borrowing – whether to purchase housing or financial investments. There is a clear connection here between global trade imbalances, inflows of cash to the USA, and the easy credit availability that fuelled both the sub-prime mortgage crisis in US housing and the boom in new financial investments financed by cheap money. This state of affairs is no longer sustainable and requires serious policy re-adjustment.

## Policy responses to trade imbalances

Trade imbalances are seen by most observers as a crucial element behind the GFC. Insofar as this is the case, what policy responses would address this issue? Several strands of thinking are evident. The first involves trade policy and relationships between currencies. US observers regard Chinese trade surpluses, in particular, as a product of cheap global Chinese exports. Chinese products are kept cheap, by the Chinese authorities refusing to allow the Chinese *yuan* to appreciate significantly against the dollar. The USA therefore looks to Chinese policy initiatives to rectify trade imbalances, while the Chinese argue that following their own national interest requires a more cautious and less radical currency appreciation. China does not regard itself as a cause of the GFC and argues that policy adjustments and reform must occur elsewhere.

Yet it is clear to all, including China, that its continuing economic development cannot simply be sustained through export-led strategies given the size of the country. Expansion of the domestic market is therefore crucial, and some shifts in this direction are evident, though previous phases of cheap domestic credit have created an asset price bubble in Chinese real estate. Tighter fiscal policies in China have a negative global effect on

Chinese imports from the rest of the world but they do not address the problem of global imbalances. In the longer term, only a reduction in surpluses arising from greater reliance on domestic growth would assist global financial re-adjustment, and this at best would only be part of any solution.

Another way of looking at the problem of structural imbalances takes a more multilateral approach, centred on alternative mechanisms for handling the trade surpluses of developing countries. Such countries, as we have seen, look for safe havens in which to place surpluses as a form of self-insurance for future financial and economic security. Location of much these surpluses in the USA in dollar denominated assets, however, creates an artificially high level for the US dollar, again making US trade re-adjustment difficult. What then if pressures to amass self-insurance surpluses were abated?

The financial journalist Martin Wolf, amongst others, has supported initiatives directed towards support for developing countries facing trade deficits and currency crises that would reduce the search for surplus and security. These include a greater role for the IMF in providing short-term non-conditional liquidity at an early stage in crises to ward off greater financial instability, building on the IMF scheme 'New Arrangements to Borrow' begun in 2008. This would need an expansion in the resources of the IMF, including an expansion in the special drawing rights (SDR) scheme run by the IMF which acts as a quasi-currency. Far more radical ideas of working towards a single world currency that would offer alternative mechanisms for re-balancing of trade relationships without financial instability have been canvassed but are not at this stage seen as politically practical. This reflects the unevenness of globalization which is far more extensive in terms of cross-border financial transactions than in monetary policy-making and financial governance.

Another way of looking at these issues argues that global imbalances may only be problematic if they inhibit sounder macro-economic policies. If US policies encouraged greater economic flexibility in response to trade competition, and if public expenditure deficits were lessened, then a more effective policy environment would better enable the USA to deal with the stresses inherent in finance markets. Neither seems likely, hence the need to perpetuate huge flows of finance.

Policy criteria here may well be seen as too focused on particular national policy settings, and insufficiently directed to more multilateral ways of thinking about how to achieve world development and poverty-reduction without financial dislocation. Martin Wolf puts it well when he argues that global finance in the lead up to the GFC had the effect of funding a rich-country real estate boom at a point when it could have been far better invested in infrastructural development in poorer countries. International monetary policy would, however, need to be reformed significantly if this were to happen.

The rise of the G20 with its wider representation of developing countries, in the aftermath of the GFC, certainly offers the possibility of a more widely drawn global debate and improved global action. In the absence of effective global macro-economic agreement among powerful economic forces such as the USA and China, the more mundane discussions at G20 level on co-ordinated approaches to global imbalances are likely to get nowhere. This, by itself, does not mean that global financial instability will continue unabated, because there are a number of additional causes of crisis that need to be taken into account. Global imbalances may therefore have helped pave the way for crisis, but they are not sufficient as an explanation for it. Even without global imbalances, financial crisis may still have occurred because of weaknesses in financial markets and in the regulatory framework surrounding it.

And the relationship between democratic accountability and global financial operations remains a fraught one. The so-called 'democracy deficit' between elite-based global institutions and democratic processes is manifest especially clearly in the area of global finance. Ordinary citizens oriented to national democratic structures feel excluded from deliberations in the G20 or IMF. There are few if any transnational democratic structures that parallel the global financial architecture. The problem of democratic deficit here is made worse by two further associated problems. One is the tendency of national politicians to operate as if unconditional national sovereignty remained intact when in reality sovereignty remains highly conditional on international processes and agreements, as well as being limited by the autonomy of global capital markets. The second problem is a lack of public education in the current shape, architecture, dynamic, and weaknesses of the global financial order. There is a huge information gap here in capacity of the general public to grasp the relevance and significance of global trade imbalances for everyday life. The void is filled by populist calls to blame the bankers and reliance on the integrity of sovereign nations to fix the mess. Blaming bankers is not, however, a solution, while individual nations are unable to produce effective policy responses without achieving higher levels of co-operative agreement than is currently evident.

## Market failure

Global trade imbalances are not the only macro-economic or structural factor at work in creating financial crisis. Some analysts hold laissez-faire models of global capitalism responsible instead. This argument may be connected with the financialization of the global economy discussed in Chapter 3. This process increased the relative importance of finance within the global economy, and hence increased the potential seriousness of market failure should anything go badly wrong. Short-term financial objectives, including the maintenance of shareholder value, also came to dominate the development of many non-financial corporations against increasing vulnerability to financial volatility. Underlying such developments, as we have seen above, was the development of a mathematically sophisticated economics of finance that treated perfect markets as necessarily efficient and claimed that risks could be identified and managed, stimulating investment strategies based on short-run arbitrage in self-regulated market arenas.

De-regulated or self-regulated markets have a long history of crisis and depression, boom and bust. Throughout recent history, a pattern of de-regulation and re-regulation is evident. This is especially true for finance because processes of credit expansion contain high levels of uncertainty over the future. Over-confidence and speculation leads to asset price 'bubbles', where the price of assets such as housing takes off in an unsustainable way. Risk is endemic in this sector, even though this is obscured during economic upswings and financial 'bubbles' when all is seen to be going well, and ideological defenders of laissez-faire look to be right – at least for those with short memories. It is this fundamental uncertainty that undermined the economics of finance and with it the whole edifice of risk-free trading in efficient markets.

Thus, the structural problem here is not simply that global finance is uncertain and unstable, but also that it is not necessarily efficient. The GFC proved once again that finance markets failed to price risk effectively into their transactions. Credit was extended by financial institutions at high rates of leverage where loans might exceed thirty times the value of assets, and where mortgages were extended to home-buyers with little realistic chance of re-payment if house prices ceased to rise each year.

When markets fail, financial value is lost, profits collapse, credit is withdrawn, and businesses collapse or go into administration. Manufacturing industry is adversely affected alongside finance. Unemployment then rises. All this happened between 2008 and 2009, at levels that were worse in the USA and Western Europe than other regions such as the Asia-Pacific. While pro-market ideologues dispute that market failure was the product of causes internal to markets, it is difficult to sustain attempts to claim that state failures are really to blame. Regulatory deficiencies are undoubtedly part of the story, as we shall see below, but it is quite unacceptable to deny that market failure happened or that finance markets have repeated problems with risk and uncertainty. They are part of the story too.

There are two major themes linking market failure in finance with wider social and economic crisis. One, as already stressed, is the endemic problem of risk and uncertainty within financial markets. The second is connected with financialization, in the sense that finance and capital markets, oriented to the short term, have had a distorting effect on product markets, oriented to the longer term. The social costs of indulging the market utopias of financial ideologues may be measured in terms of economic volatility, diminished growth rates, crises in housing finance in countries such as the USA, and post-crisis restrictions on creditworthiness.

## Responses to market failure

How then may market failure be addressed in policy reform?

One obvious response is better regulation – something that we shall move on to consider below. Before doing that, it is worthwhile looking briefly at a more general sociological perspective, to identify some of the broader social aspects of the problem.

Sociology views the ideological notion of free-standing markets and laissez-faire policy as encouraging a profound and pathological differentiation of economy from society. Rather than markets always providing the goods which are then allocated according to the cultural preferences of consumers, there are occasions when markets generate economic bads that generate political and cultural instability, which, in turn disrupts social cohesion. If markets under certain conditions produce pathological outcomes, they should not be written off altogether because under other conditions they may generate economic growth, advancing the aggregate social welfare of the planet more efficiently than other systems – if efficiency is measured in terms of levels of productivity. So what conditions work?

One way of thinking about this is to consider the embedding or re-embedding of markets into society, that is, through the creation of social markets. These have been defined in different ways, but a common thread running through them is the idea that social considerations should exist alongside economic imperatives. While it is conventional to think of political systems intervening in already existing markets, to meet social obligations funded through taxation and borrowing, this may be insufficient to permit re-embedding of markets into society. This is often when markets directly and manifestly produce bads, such as low wages, abusive work conditions or environmental pollution, bads that should be directly tackled at source. But it is also where characteristic structures and cultures of market-based decision-making fail to recognize antisocial practices, which are more latent and less manifest in their operations. Short-term profit-seeking based on highly risky investment practices is one example. Another is the creation of personal incentive arrangements that simply reward profit when made, but do not penalize loss on a proportionate and reciprocal basis when it is incurred.

Responses to market failure, therefore, may operate at the level of changing not only social and cultural norms but also expectations about what should be done and how it should be achieved, as well as at the more conventional level of institutional re-structuring.

Relevant examples of social and cultural change involve matters such as the curriculum of business school training, professional codes of conduct in financial trading, and governance processes within financial institutions. Cultural change is not irrelevant to averting market failure, because it is clearly of importance to issues such as the lack of sufficient emphasis on business ethics within the curriculum of business schools over the last two decades, or the limited scope of corporate social responsibility schemes within the short-term worlds of finance markets and market players. Yet one perennial problem with this kind of thinking is that it is often vague and exhortatory, lacking a specific normative thrust that institutions and financial actors may take up.

Paul Woolley, writing in *The Future of Finance* (2010), an important volume published by the London School of Economics, provides a more specific and elaborate example of desirable normative reform in finance. This involves what he calls 'a manifesto for giant funds'. The aim is to produce a normative strategy for large institutional investors that is designed both to stabilize markets and increase long-term returns by avoiding high-risk investments that lead to market failure. His interpretation of where finance went wrong focuses on the familiar themes of the mispricing of risk, but he links this with a structural feature of finance to do with the relationship between principals (i.e. investors) and agents (i.e. financial intermediaries such as traders).

This relationship went wrong during the period of financialization because agents gained excessive autonomy from investors, allowing them to devise and trade in complex derivative financial products that few investors understood. The vast fees paid to agents therefore amount to rent capture by agents rather than an efficient market-based allocation of returns to successful trading firms. A key remedy to prevent this happening again is therefore a more pro-active stance by investors, especially those giant 'public, pension, and charitable' funds that have an interest in long-term returns.

Woolley's manifesto offers a way of promoting this agenda around a number of key principles. These include the following:

- Adopt a long-term approach to investing based on long-term dividend flows, rather than momentum-based strategies that rely on short-term price changes.
- Cap annual turnover of portfolios at 30 per cent.
- Understand that all the tools currently used to determine (investment) policy objectives and implementation are based on the discredited theory of efficient markets.
- Do not sanction the purchase of 'structured', untraded or synthetic products.
- Do not pay performance fees (or only pay on long-term performance).
- Insist on total transparency by managers with respect to their strategies, costs, leverage, and trading.
- Allow public scrutiny of fund compliance with these policies.

This manifesto is worth quoting at some length because it indicates some ways in which the pathological and dysfunctional separation of finance from broader considerations such as long-term financial sustainability, trust in managers' trading procedures and public transparency may be addressed and reformed. Markets are neither efficient left to themselves, nor do they guarantee the social legitimacy of global finance. However, it is possible to conceive of specific normative and procedural changes that could be implemented within finance that do not wholly rely on external political regulation. This means that advocates of such changes bypass the obvious criticism that states and state-regulation can 'fail' too.

This does not mean that regulation always fails, any more than markets always fail. Nor does it mean that regulation could not help underwrite normative and procedural change. Woolley gives two examples. One involves the approval of new financial products. These should not be approved simply because they claim to increase liquidity or complete markets. The second involves taxable treatment of funds. In the UK, at least, these may be tax exempt, providing they invest rather than trade. When a high proportion of the portfolio is turned over by fund managers in any given year, this begins to look suspiciously like trading, yet is rarely penalized through loss of tax exemption. Regulators in his view should be more pro-active in this area, and the norm of a cap of 30 per cent turn-over each year would seem a reasonable indicator of an investment strategy geared to long-term returns rather than short-run speculation.

Woolley's argument that performance fees should not be paid to traders and fund managers engages with a matter of huge public interest; namely, the remuneration of financial service providers. While much populist anger has been directed against levels of pay, it may be more relevant for the prevention of market failure to consider the structure of pay. There are two interrelated issues here. One is the incentive to engage in high-risk but potentially high-return activity created by reward of short-term invest-ment success rather than long-term economic returns. A second closely linked problem is the tendency to reward success but not to penalize failure. While leading traders have made huge bonuses in good times through risky behaviour, the losses incurred in the GFC did not generate a corresponding direct penalty – rather the public purse picked up most of the losses. The perverse incentives in this structure of pay create dangers for global finance as a whole and are distinct from the issue of levels of pay, which may violate community notions of fairness, and which can be dealt with through the tax system.

The problem of uncertainty-induced market failure is therefore an issue that requires recognition not only by public investment and pension funds, but also in wider public policy debates. This is partly a question of identifying ways of anticipating and averting failure, and partly a question of allowing broader social and political considerations into the worlds of global finance. This is perhaps easier for central bankers, who, as we have seen, may bring historical memory and intuitive judgements of what works into play. It may be far harder for traders whose increasingly screen-based trading horizons are very short term, backed up by automatic trading programmes. In between these two layers of the financial world are the various financial institutions such as banks, insurance companies, and pension funds. Some of these fit into Woolley's category of principals who have the capacity to mandate investment goals and procedures. However, for investment banks, or mixed-function banks who perform commercial and trading activities, the position is very different.

The highest profits in banking in the lead-up to the GFC came precisely from short-run arbitrage using derivatives that are targeted by Woolley as short term and based on the false promise of risk-free trading in efficient markets. Remedies against a repeat of market-failure in global finance have therefore extended to questions of how to limit the disruptive consequences of investment banking failures as manifest in the GFC with the demise of Lehman Brothers and huge bail-outs for other banks such as Goldman Sachs.

The most widely canvassed remedy is to somehow separate commercial and investment banking in order to protect the credit extended to households and smaller business from the consequences of credit collapse brought on by investment banking failures. Since this is unlikely to arise spontaneously from the banking system itself, it looms large as a major feature of regulatory reform to which we now turn.

## Policy and regulatory failure

Poor public policy and poor regulation have been canvassed as major causes of the GFC requiring policy re-think and regulatory reform. Some balance is therefore required in combining an awareness of market failure with policy and regulatory failure as co-present causes of crisis rather than opting for one or the other to fit ideological prejudices. And the corollary of this kind of balance is a parallel recognition that not everything about finance markets is bad or dysfunctional, just as not everything about monetary policy and financial regulation is fundamentally defective.

Finance market intermediation has had a large measure of success in creating long-term credit from the typically shorter-term perspectives of investors. This in turn has helped stimulate economic growth and technological innovation through the continuing evolution of capital markets. Policies of low interest rates, other things being equal, have made a contribution to the avoidance of inflation preserving the value of savings and pensions, while equally lowering cost burdens on business loans and mortgages. Financial regulation meanwhile has learnt something from previous crises in terms of identifying institutional weakness in banking structures associated with inadequate capital reserves, as well as beginning the reform of these processes. That regulation in this area ultimately failed to prevent crisis is in part because financial institutions did not implement prudential regulation, as much as any fault in the regulatory structure itself.

The leading candidate for public policy failure in the lead up to the GFC is that monetary policy set by central bankers was too easy. This charge is laid especially at the door of the US Federal Reserve led up until 2006 by Alan Greenspan and more recently by Ben Bernanke. The argument here is that short-term interest rates were kept low in a manner that was too inflexible. While positive in many respects, this orientation to monetary policy meant that little attempt was made to use policy levers to prevent or at least put a check to asset price bubbles. Rather than a pro-active policy of 'leaning against the wind' as practised, for example by the Australian Reserve Bank in relation to potential real estate bubbles, Greenspan preferred to use monetary policy to 'mop up' after markets had come much closer to bubble-induced crisis. Bernanke seems to be continuing in this mould, looking more to regulation to avert future volatility and crisis than to stepping in earlier.

In essence, this approach reduces central bank policy to price stability. It represents a kind of minimalist policy perspective. The rationale behind it is that excessive intervention to prick asset price bubbles before they reach extreme proportions could potentially weaken growth and impose unnecessary economic costs. Yet the obvious criticism of this position is that merely mopping up after bubbles burst fails to avert costs of asset price collapse, which in the case of the GFC far exceeded the costs of an earlier pre-emptive move. The point here is that the cost to growth of some monetary tightening before asset price bubbles gain too much momentum may be rather limited, and most probably less than when momentum is greater and bubbles have burst.

A broader approach to monetary policy is, however, unlikely to be a sufficient remedy by itself to avert future crisis, especially as so many regulatory failures are evident in the lead up to the GFC.

The sociologist John Braithwaite (2008) has characterized the contemporary global economy not in terms of financialization, but as regulatory capitalism. Cutting through debates about the need for greater regulation as against de-regulation, his argument is that markets never generate spontaneous order by themselves but rely on some kind of regulation, whether public or private in form. This perspective provides a way of cutting through misleading ideologically debates that use highly rhetorical language about regulation, including the conceptual sleight of hand that regards de-regulation as no regulation, and the conflation of regulation with public initiative alone. As it happens, the GFC witnessed regulatory failure both with respect to public agencies and with private self-regulatory initiatives, the two of which are often closely interconnected.

Regulatory failure associated with the GFC has been associated with both general features of global finance and specific features of the regulatory framework in particular nations, notably the USA, but also the UK. One of the most serious general problems was a lack of adequate capital in the banking system. This under-capitalization of banks was reflected both by the scale of losses entailed and by the huge size of public bail-outs to keep many major global banks afloat. Under-capitalization might be thought to represent a private failure of inadequate provisioning by banks in relation to the liabilities they took on. Sole focus on this argument would, however, understate problems of public regulatory failure in the global rules of capital adequacy for banks developed through the so-called Basel Accords.

Basel is the home of the central bankers' bank – the Bank for International Settlements which has been tasked over the last thirty-five years with greater monitoring and supervision of cross-border capital movements, including a sense of the capital it is prudent for banks to have available to weather crises. This initiative represented a belated global regulatory response to the globalization of banking and financial markets which previously were left to national regulators. After a period of deliberating over the principles of banking regulation, the Basel Committee for banking supervision developed three successive Accords. Basel 1 dating from 1988 emerged in the aftermath of the stock market collapse of 1987. This first Accord focused on problems of inadequate capital held by banks, which reduced their capacity to weather crisis. Basel 1 determined capital adequacy in terms of a set ratio of the securest kind of bank capital (such as shareholders equity or home government bonds) to its total assets (taking into account the risk profile in the various types of assets). This ratio was broadly determined at 8 per cent.

This kind of regulation, designed to secure adequate capital reserves taking risk into account, was largely evaded by many banks. Further attempts to produce more effective capital adequacy requirements led to Basel 2 dating from 2004. This new Accord emerged after further financial crises in the 1990s. It now gave financial regulators greater flexibility in making judgements about the adequacy of capital held by particular banks, but did not revise the basic ratio or the kinds of capital that could be counted. This meant significant regulatory weaknesses were still intact as the GFC was to demonstrate.

A key weakness of the system was a pro-cyclical bias. This means that this structure of supervision encouraged banks to hold too little capital in an upswing when risks appeared lower, and too much capital in a down-swing when risks appeared more evident. The net effect of pro-cyclicality was that credit expansion in an upswing was not backed by sufficient assets, while in an economic downswing credit was contracted too sharply to meet risk-based capital adequacy ratios. In this latter case, the scale of downswings was made worse by the capital adequacy regime. These arrangements were therefore a contributory cause to the worsening of the depth and severity of the GFC.

Underlying such weaknesses are several further problems. First, capital adequacy levels were still too low. Second, assessment of the quality of capital in relation to risk was inadequate. This relates to a third major problem; namely, that risk was assessed on an individual basis – bank by bank – using a variety of procedures, rather than at the level of the system as a whole. Amongst other things, this individualistic approach failed to take into account the complex web of risks involved in dealings between banks and financial institutions, through instruments such as credit default swaps, discussed in Chapter 2. However, the failure to take a system-wide approach to risk is clearly a problem of public regulation that contributed to the GFC.

Further problems of regulation involve variable compliance with Basel 2, which US banks had not signed up to. Their own capital adequacy ratios were often far lower than 8 per cent, as low as 4 per cent in some cases. Problems of low compliance are a product of weak public supervision as well as private avoidance of a broader social responsibility to play their part in securing financial stability.

Another important dimension to the GFC is the distinction between capital adequacy and liquidity. An everyday way of thinking of liquidity is 'ready money', that is, assets immediately available to make transactions, such as servicing debts. Global finance based on credit requires both adequate capital reserves in financial institutions and liquidity so that day-to-day transactions can be met. In the GFC, liquidity dried up as institutions found they could not re-finance short-term loans when they expired and fresh loans were needed. In the USA, Bear Stearns had to be saved when its cash ran dry, Lehman Brothers then collapsed, and Goldman Sachs came close to running out of money.

A key problem here is that regulators have spent far more time thinking about capital adequacy and too little about liquidity. In a sense, financial institutions left it to central bankers to ensure liquidity, especially since holding assets in liquid form offers institutions a very low return. Regulators, however, had not included liquidity within the Basel Accords, and this clearly reduced the buffers that might otherwise have been put in place to secure greater financial resilience. Even so, inadequate liquidity was not a fundamental cause of the GFC, since it was the high rates of leverage on loans that created much of the difficulty, itself linked as we have seen to the culture of finance.

In addition to these general problems of global regulation, other more specific problems emerged in particular national settings. Many elements of finance continue to be regulated at a national, and sometimes even a sub-national level, such as the state jurisdictions in federally organized nations.

National regulation may not always be the optimal level for addressing key features of global finance which require co-operation and co-ordination, such as capital adequacy ratios for banks engaged in cross-border transactions. However, key nations such as the USA and UK had not, by the eve of the GFC, developed integrated or co-ordinated systems of domestic financial regulation. This mattered greatly because both were the home of world-leading financial centres in Wall Street and the City of London.

The regulatory system in the USA has generally been singled out as having the most significant levels of weakness. This is largely because it did not function as a co-ordinated system. It was composed rather as a complex set of separate regulatory domains, further weakened by holes in sectors such as insurance where federal public regulation was non-existent. The US preference for separate regulators for each sub-section of finance made it almost impossible to co-ordinate action to prevent crisis, in terms of both information-sharing and co-ordination of action. Banks, insurance, stock markets, and the public housing mortgage system operated by Freddie Mac and Fannie Mae, were regulated separately, sometimes at state level and sometimes federally. This partly explains why the full significance of finance sector exposures to the sub-prime mortgage crisis was not appreciated earlier, and why system-level risk in the financial sector as a whole was not evident to most observers until too late.

If public regulators failed in the various ways indicated above, this does not necessarily mean that the market would have done all right if only regulation had been better. This is because market self-regulation failed too. This is partly a matter of poor corporate governance and oversight of banking and credit practices. Many corporate leaders did not fully understand the new complex derivative products or systems of insurance surrounding them, partly because lending policies operated on leverage ratios that far exceeded prudent levels. Derivatives were themselves both poorly self-regulated and poorly regulated, if at all by public regulators. While it may be true that money gravitates to the least well-regulated sectors, both private and public regulators bear responsible for the dire consequences. In the private sector, the debt-rating agencies, seemed to perceive nothing much going wrong until crisis hit, while the lucrative momentum behind leveraged derivative trading was not properly scrutinized by managers or accountants. Public scrutiny and regulation was largely non-existent.

## Towards more effective regulation

What fresh regulatory initiatives are therefore required to deal with the GFC and the future economic sustainability of global finance?

A unifying theme in the discussion of both market and regulatory failure is the lack of any system-wide capacity to understand the build-up of risk. This failure applies to the mathematical models that traders believed could price-risk into market transactions, to the practice of corporations to calculate risks for their own firm alone, and to the failure of public regulators at national and global levels to understand risk. To put the problem in the more technical language discussed in Chapter 5, the problem for finance markets is one of uncertainty as much as risk. The distinction between uncertainty and risk, as we have seen in earlier chapters, makes it possible to assess how far problems derive from unknowable contingencies that we cannot measure or predict, as against those contingencies whose probability can be reliably calculated and managed. The priority then for more effective regulation is not simply a better structure for the management for risk, but also to determine how to plan for uncertainty.

Andrew Haldane of the Bank of England argues that global finance operating as a cross-border network of nodes and linkages is particularly vulnerable to extreme and uncertain events. This is partly because of the intense scale of inter-connections across the globe, and also because risk hitherto has been calculated on an atomistic level within the nodes rather than across the linkages.

Re-stabilizing a vulnerable system of this kind requires a range of initiatives. Some require better information of network-wide risk rather than risk within particular nodes. After the collapse of hedge fund Long Term Capital Management (LTCM) in 1998, the Bank for International Settlements began to collect cross-border banking statistics. After the GFC, there is a need to extend this to financial flows in general, including non-bank institutions. This would, however, have to have a better grasp of the many off-balance sheet financial transactions that securitization has spawned. And beyond better information, the improved analysis of risk requires new forms of analysis that operate beyond the level of individual firms to that of financial networks and the financial system as a whole. Haldane looks here to network theory in general, and measures of robustness developed by statisticians around characteristic patterns of network interaction. But he also looks to epidemiology in biology, noting that disease epidemics feature a relatively few high-risk super-spreaders with high numbers of network linkages, which are disproportionately responsible for contagion. This model might well be applied in finance where a few large financial institutions, such as Lehman Brothers, may play a disproportionate role in spreading crisis.

These analytical points have great implications for reform of global financial regulation. Much emphasis has been placed here on tightening the capital adequacy ratios to which global banks are subject. The BIS and the Financial Stability Board, as expert regulatory advisors to the G20 nations, have recently been involved in the development of Basel Accord 3. The latest regulatory changes included higher and more robust levels of capital adequacy, including an increase from 2 per cent to 7 per cent in the highest quality (tier one shareholder equity) capital – albeit phased in over eight years. There are also encouragements to operate a higher level of provision in the good years as a counter-cyclical strategy against future crisis. Surprisingly, however, there is far less regulation of the leverage ratios banks may operate. Under Basel 3, these may still be as high as 33.33 times tier one capital.

It is also not clear that Basel 3 addresses Haldane's point that particular institutions may need specific regulatory attention due to the scale and vulnerability of their activities. Macro-prudential regulation does not address this problem. Historical problems with individual institutions were handled privately by other bankers, while in the twentieth-century central banks have played a more major role. Indeed, there is some indication that larger banks in the run up to the GFC expected public help if they ever got into difficulty and operated inadequate capital buffers accordingly. This in turn raises the problem of whether some institutions are too big to fail, and whether it was a mistake to let Lehman Brothers go under. The case for allowing failure, at least on rare occasions, centres on problems of moral hazard and wider political and social considerations, including finite limits to the public purse.

The moral hazard argument is that financial institutions should not be encouraged to pursue unduly risky courses of action, confident that they will always be bailed out if things go very wrong. Private sector institutions, especially the larger ones, must accept market penalties for faulty decision-making including the mis-pricing of risk. Public support cannot be unlimited. Excessive levels of support, as recently provided by the Irish state to its own banks, risk bringing on a fiscal crisis of the state on top of the GFC. This in turn creates highly politicized dilemmas for democratic nations. Adequate state expenditure to support banks may require cut-backs to other kinds of public expenditure, risking social conflict. Recourse to increased taxation would be extremely unpopular, and make crises worse, at a time that risks of default make borrowing on the sovereign debt market more expensive for governments. Once again there is need for a sociology of finance that goes beyond the internal economics of markets in order to analyse the linkages between markets, states, citizens, and cultural expectations made of financial institutions and governments.

## Conclusion

In this chapter we have applied a broader sociological to the analysis of the GFC and what should be done about it. At the time of writing, the sovereign debt crises in European countries is still spreading and stock markets remain volatile and fearful. While each displays features particular to the nation in question – such as the chaotic state of Greek public finances across recent history – there are common themes in play. The GFC, which began as a sub-prime mortgage crisis, and developed into a full-scale crisis of global credit and capital markets, now continues as a crisis of sovereign indebtedness. In Greece, though not Ireland, this spills over beyond parliamentary conflict into social conflict in the streets. Changes in economic policy and regulatory structures discussed above may offer some longer-term success in averting or limiting the impact of future crises but they will not resolve short-term socio-political discontent or restore the reputation of the finance industry, bankers, and regulators.

The re-legitimization of global finance is not simply a matter of waiting for street conflict to subside, but requires a greater awareness of the democracy deficit and information divide that separates the worlds and cultures of finance from wider populations. This divide applies to all aspects of globalization, as much as the globalization of finance in particular. The world of trading rooms, arbitrage, and derivatives, and the interest-rate setting and macro-prudential activities of central bankers are not well understood in the world outside by legislators let alone citizens. Bridging this gap is not only a matter of demonstrating market and regulatory success in achieving economic advance without crisis, but also requires a better architecture of democratic transparency to allow more informed democratic deliberation about its purposes, its strengths, and limits.

Underlying this endeavour is a set of critical questions, namely 'is economic globalization compatible with democracy? If so, is this democracy as practised in the slow-moving worlds of national politics, or is greater democratization of global regulatory bodies required?'.

One aspect of this that demands greater and more urgent attention than hitherto is improved education – in terms of both public education of citizens and specialist education in schools and universities. Improved public education would require continuous disclosure requirements in relation to all capital and money markets on the model of the disclosure requirements imposed on many share markets. It also requires a greater emphasis on finance – corporate and governmental as well as household – within curricula. If citizens were better aware of the relationships between government expenditure and bond markets, or of the intrinsic risks and uncertainties involved in credit provision, their expectations and capacities to realize their objectives would be greatly enhanced. To the objection that this is simply too technical or hard to achieve, the obvious rejoinder is that analysis of improved information flows would be enhanced if the education of graduates and school-leavers provided a greater emphasis on finance in the curriculum. This, in turn, following the analysis offered in this book, should be inter-disciplinary, placing economic insights in a broader sociological and scientific framework.

This book is written precisely to advance these educative functions, demonstrating that finance need not be technically complex, and that analytical depth need not be sacrificed in the search to write accessibly. This volume is dedicated then to the principle of deliberative democracy and to the hope that its practitioners may feel emboldened to restructure global finance, even in the midst of its darkest days.

# GLOSSARY

*Bonds*:
Financial products based on the payment of a sum of money to a government or business in return for future regular income streams. Bonds can be sold on by purchasers to others.

*Collateralized Debt Obligations*:
An investment product backed by a pool of financial assets, such as bonds or loans, that vary in the risks associated with them.

*Credit Default Swaps*:
Financial institutions can take out insurance against the failure of debtors to repay loans, that is, default. This credit default insurance can, however, be traded or swapped, such that institutions may hold credit default instruments applying to potential defaults on the loan book of other institutions.

*Derivatives*:
Financial products whose value is derived from the value of some other financial entity, such as a stock market index, or an estimate of the future value of a particular share price derived from its current value.

*Embeddedness/Embedding*:
Sociological concepts that refer to the way in which economic processes are set within and dependent on wider social processes, even if this is not necessarily acknowledged by market participants.

*Financialization*:

An increase in the importance of finance within the economy as a whole.

*Investment Banking*:

This is where banks conduct investment activity on their own account, as distinct from commercial banking, based on the provision of loans and transaction services for customers. Investment banking, especially where it is based on high rates of leverage (see below), is more high risk and high return, but can, in a crisis, jeopardize the retail banking deposits of small depositors taken during the course of normal commercial banking.

*Legitimacy*:

A sociological concept referring to acceptance of the authority of particular institutions (such as banks), or of ways of organizing social life (such as markets, payment of bankers bonuses and so forth). Acceptance can fall short of complete agreement with the institution or practice in question, but minimally must involve practical compliance.

*Leverage*:

Technically, this means the taking on or issuing of loans to finance economic activity, usually secured against a set of assets. De-leveraging means reduction in loans previously taken on or issued.

*Risk*:

The term carries a number of meanings. As used in this study, it is contrasted with uncertainty. Risk refers to future contingencies that it is possible to anticipate and whose probability can in some sense be calculated, allowing planning for the future. If markets can measure risk, they can then price risk into the market value of financial products. Risk here is distinct from uncertainty which cannot be measured. It is also distinct from the uses of risk by the sociologist Ulrich Beck, who sees risk as combining adverse contingency with environmental and species hazard.

*Securitization*:

The process whereby financial flows (e.g. loan payments) received by a financial institution secured on some asset, such as houses or a car, can be packaged together into a pool and then sold on to other investors.

*Social Differentiation*:
A sociological concept referring to the separation of distinct spheres or component parts of society from one another, usually reflected in specialized institutions performing distinct functions. This study deals with the differentiation of economy from society. Differentiation generally raises problems of system integration and social cohesion.

*Sub-prime mortgages*:
Mortgages extended to high-risk clients; for example, those with no assets and/or no job.

*Uncertainty*:
In a technical sense, this refers to future contingencies that cannot be predicted or anticipated, and thus reliably integrated into the planning and management of businesses and governments. Extreme events are an example. (See also *Risk*.)

# FURTHER READING

The concept of a financial system is defined in R.C. Merton and Z. Bodie (1995) 'A Conceptual Framework for Analyzing the Financial Environment', in D.B. Crane *et al.* (eds), *The Global Financial System: A Functional Perspective*, Boston: Harvard University Business School Press, pp. 3–33.

The contemporary operations of global finance, up to and including the global financial crisis, are ably discussed in A. Turner (2010) 'What Do Banks Do?', in A. Turner *et al.* (ed.) *The Future of Finance: The LSE Report*, London: London School of Economic and Political Science, pp. 3–63.

D. McKenzie (2006) *An Engine, Not a Camera: How Financial Models Shape Markets*, Boston: MIT Press.

Important contributions to the study of regulation include: J. Braithwaite and P. Drahos (2000) *Global Business Regulation*, Cambridge: Cambridge University Press.

J. Braithwaite (2008) *Regulatory Capitalism*, Cheltenham: Elgar.

Important studies in the history of global finance include N. Ferguson (2008) *The Ascent of Money*, London: Allen Lane.

C. Kindleberger (1978) *Manias, Panics and Crashes: A History of Financial Crises*, London: Macmillan.

C.M. Reinhart and K. Rogoff (2009) *This Time is Different: Eight Centuries of Financial Folly*, Princeton: Princeton University Press.

Aspects of financialization are explored in G. Epstein (ed.) (2005) *Financialization and the Global Economy*, Cheltenham: Elgar.

A range of publications including: S. Sassen (1996) *Losing Control? Sovereignty in an Age of Globalization*, New York: Columbia University Press.

——(2005) *Cities in a World Economy*, Thousand Oaks: Pine Forge Press, explores both the social geography of global finance and the problems of loss of democratic sovereignty.

A broad set of essays covering many aspects of the sociology of financial markets is available in K. Knorr Cetina and A. Preda (eds.) (2005) *The Sociology of Financial Markets*, Oxford: Oxford University Press.

Sociological insights into the worlds of financial traders may be obtained from the work of K. Knorr Cetina and U. Bruegger (2002) 'Global Microstructures: the Virtual Societies of Financial Markets', *American Journal of Sociology*, 107(4), 905–50.

D. Buenza and D. Stark (2004) 'Tools of the Trade: the Socio-Technology of Arbitrage in a Wall Street Trading Room', *Industrial and Corporate Change*, 13(2), 369–400.

Central bankers' worlds are very ably explored in J. Pixley (2004) *Emotions in Finance*, Cambridge: Cambridge University Press, with particular reference to uncertainty and trust.

Key theoretical resources in the understanding of how markets, states, and cultures interconnect are available in M. Weber (1968) *Economy and Society*, 2 vols, Berkeley: University of California Press.

K. Polanyi (1944) *The Great Transformation*, Boston: Beacon Press.

M. Granovetter (1985) 'Economic Action and Social Structure: The Problem of Embeddedness', *American Journal of Sociology*, 89, 481–510.

For the analytical scope of economic sociology, see R. Swedberg (2003) *Principles of Economic Sociology*, Princeton: Princeton University Press.

Insights into the psychology of markets are available in R. Shiller (2000) *Irrational Exuberance*, Princeton: Princeton University Press.

Very helpful introductions in the causes and policy options available to resolve problems highlighted in the GFC are available in M. Wolf (2009), *Fixing Global Finance: How to Curb Financial Crises in the 21st Century*, Newhaven: Yale University Press.

H. Davies (2010) *The Financial Crisis: Who Is To Blame?* Cambridge: Polity Press.

P. Woolley (2010) 'Why are Financial Markets Inefficient and Exploitative – And a Suggested Remedy', in A. Turner *et al.* (eds) see above, Chapter 3.

# WEB RESOURCES

The general dimensions of cross-border financial flows are available from the Bank for International Settlements (www.bis.org/statistics/index.htm).

Individual financial institutions also provide information on their own global activities, though some offer a far more direct and transparent approach than others.

The most helpful websites include the leading global bond dealers, Pimco (www.pimco.com/en/Pages/default.aspx), banks such as Barclays (www.barclays.com), then navigate to 'Barclays Worldwide', and Credit Suisse (www.credit-suisse.com/who_we_are/en). Morgan Stanley Smith Barney provide interesting information on investment banking (see www.morganstanley.com/institutional/invest_bank/index.html).

Global insurance is well represented by Lloyds of London (www.lloyds.com) whose website also provides interesting insights into challenges posed by global risk. While Moodys, the debt ratings agency, in its own website (www.moodys.com) outlines its thinking on the risks involved in the sovereign debts of nations.

Corporate websites clearly try to represent their activities in the most favourable light possible. More independent judgements are available in some specialist financial journalism, though it is always worth checking whether particular writers make explicit where they hold financial interests in companies under review. Specialist websites of the Financial Times of London (www.ft.com) and the Australian Financial Review (www.afr.com.au) offer well-informed analytical material, but much of this is on a subscription basis only. Reuters (www.reuters.com) and the *Wall Street Journal* (www.wsj.com) are more accessible.

The personal websites of economists and financial journalists are very useful. Good examples include those of the economist John Kay (www.johnkay.com), fellow economist Joseph Stiglitz (www.josephstiglitz.com) and the world's pre-eminent financial journalist Martin Wolf, whose columns appear within the Financial Times of London (www.ft.com). There are also tens of thousands of financial blogs offering varying degrees of expertise, many focused on individual day traders rather than large professional traders. The best site for financial commentary is Reuters (www.reuters.com – select 'opinion').

Financial regulation at a global level is available within the International Monetary Fund (www.imf.org) and the Bank for International Settlements (www.bis.org). The key role of the Federal Reserve Bank in the USA may be tracked in its website (www.federalreserve.gov). Other important central bank websites include the Bank of England (www.bankofengland.co.uk) and the European Central Bank (www.ecb.int). These sites include discussion and execution of policy and regulatory decisions as well as analytical observations. On the Bank of England website, the papers by Andrew Haldane, director of financial stability, are particularly interesting on questions of risk and uncertainty, see for example 'The $100 Billion Question' (www.bankofengland.co.uk/publications/speeches/2010/speech433.pdf).

# INDEX

Accounting practises, 46
Africa, 4, 50
AIG insurance, 25
Amsterdam, 37
Amsterdam Exchange Bank, 37
ancient Babylon, 35
arbitrage, 20–21, 60, 63
asset price bubbles, 49, 52, 54, 89,
   98–99
Asia, 4, 35. 39, 50, 89
Asia-Pacific, 93
Australian Reserve Bank, 98
Austria, 38

Bank for International Settlements,
   9, 14, 29–30, 67–68, 86, 99–100,
   103, 112
bank notes, 37
Bank of Amsterdam, 37
Bank of England, 9, 37, 41, 68, 85, 113
banking; history of, 36–54; internal
   hierarchies, 61; investment and
   commercial banking, 19–20,
   38–40, 53, 61, 97, 108
Banque de France, 41

Barclays, 9, 20, 112
Bardi family, 36
Barings, 38, 58
Basel Capital Accords, 30, 99–101
Bear Stearns, 101
Beck, Ulrich, 51
bills of exchange, 35, 37
Black Swans, 51
Black–Scholes–Merton formulae,
   61–64, 75
Bloomberg, 9
bond markets, 17, 26–28, 38–39
bonds, 17–19, 37–39, 88, 107
Braithwaite, John, 13, 23, 41, 99, 110
Brazil, 38
Bretton Woods institutions, 12, 42
business education, 94–95

Callon, Michel, 68–69
capitalism, 6, 13, 23, 43–47, 54, 99
central banks and bankers, 30–31,
   41, 64–67
central European industrialization,
   44, 46
cheques, 36–37

Chicago Board of Trade, 9, 40–41, 58
Chicago Board Options Exchange, 62
Chicago Mercantile Exchange,
    40–41
China, 4, 35–36, 38, 53, 88–91
City of London, 9, 37–39, 41, 102
Collateralized debt obligations
    (CDO's), 19, 25–6, 31, 107
Credit default swaps (CDS's), 40, 107
currency crises, 49–50

Davies, Howard, 87,
democracy deficit, 47–48, 67,
    91–92, 105–106
Denmark, 38
deregulation; arguments in
    favour and against, 39–40,
    85–86, 92–93; problems of
    definition, 13
derivatives, 16, 39, 61–64, 67, 102, 107
Dojima rice market, 40
Dow Jones share index, 16
Drahos, Peter, 41
Dutch East India Company, 38

economics; general approach to
    markets, 71–75; limits to
    economists' analyses of finance, 2,
    54, 56, 61–70, 76–78
economics of finance, 61–64, 74–75
electronic trading systems, 9, 21,
    58–59
embedding and dis-embedding of
    economy and sociaty, 82–83,
    94, 107
epidemiology and the modelling of
    crises, 104
Europe, 1, 4, 27, 35, 38, 51–3, 82,
    87, 93
European Central Bank, 9, 26,
    68, 113
European Union, 68, 86

Ferguson, Niall, 34, 110
finance; and cross-border trade,
    35–6, 53; and credit, 13–14,
19–24, 34–5, 74, 93; and crisis,
    1–2, 11–12, 38, 44, 49–54, 57,
    62–64, 66–67, 75–76, 87; and
    emotions, 6. 56–57, 59, 65–66,
    77–78, 86; and empire, 38, 44;
    and extreme events, 51, 63,
    75–76, 84; and intermediation,
    16–17, 21–3, 98; and market
    knowledge, 61–70, 74–75; and
    law, 11–12, 23–4, 35, 42; and
    liquidity, 30–31, 53, 64, 101; and
    mortgages, 19, 21–22, 29, 52; and
    national sovereignty, 1, 27–8, 50,
    105–106; and networks, 23,
    31–32, 58–59, 66, 68, 103–4; and
    problems of legitimacy, 3, 10–11,
    86–87, 105–106, 108; and
    perverse incentives for traders,
    96–97; and psychology, 56,
    61–64, 66–67, 78–79; and
    regulation, 1, 7, 13, 23, 28–33,
    41–42, 53, 68, 73–74, 85, 95–97;
    and the 'real economy', 14; and
    the theory of the firm, 46; and
    trust, 31–32, 46, 57, 59, 82; as
    part of society, 3–4, 9–13, 67–84,
    105–6; culture of , 55–70, 85–6,
    94–95; financial products, 8–33;
    history of, 2, 6, 11, 29, 34–54;
    importance of people within it,
    5–6, 31–32, 55–70; importance of
    reputation, 64–67, 86; institutions
    of finance, 5, 8–33, 35–54;
    inter-bank lending, 24; key
    functions of, 6, 13–33; power of,
    47–49, 77; principal-agent
    problems, 95–96; social geography
    of, 6, 34–54; sociological
    approach towards, 2–3, 6–7,
    10–13, 32, 54, 62. 67–70, 77–84,
    86–7, 93–94, 105–106
Financial Services Agency (UK), 28,
Financial Stability Board, 104
financialization, 45–46, 77, 93, 97, 108
First World War, 51
Ford Motors, 45

foreign exchange markets, 58
France, 47
Freddie Mac and Fannie Mae, 102
futures markets, 15–16, 40–41

G7, G8 and G20, 42, 68, 86, 91, 104
General Electric and GE Finance, 45
General Motors, 45
Genoa, 37
Germany, 51–52
Global Financial Crisis (GFC); general
    features of, 1, 4–5, 11–12, 17–18,
    21–22, 26, 29, 38, 45–49, 53–5; 68,
    70–71, 73, 76, 82, 85–6, 91, 93,
    97–98, 100, 103; causes of, 21–22,
    25–6, 32, 47, 49–54, 67–70,
    87–89, 92–93, 97–100
Global cities, 9
globalization; and finance, 4–5, 24,
    43–47, 50–51, 53, 58, 64–68,
    88–90; and national sovereignty,
    4–5, 24, 47–48, 64, 85–6; and
    political democracy, 5, 47–48,
    95–96; and power, 4, 47–48;
    definition, 4, 8; history of, 34–54
Gold standard, 42, 52
Goldman Sachs, 9, 20, 97
Government debt, 26–28, 31
Great Depression, 4, 11, 51–54
Greece, 4, 50, 53, 105
Greenspan, Alan, 66, 78, 98

Haldane, Andrew, 47, 69, 103–4, 113
Hambros, 38
Harvey, David, 43
hedge funds, 20, 62–3,
Hilferding, Rudolf, 43–44, 46
historical sociology of finance, 34–54
Hong King stock exchange, 39

India, 35
inflation crises, 50
insurance services, 15, 25, 40
International Association of
    Investment Bankers, 9,
international monetary system, 12, 52

International Monetary Fund (IMF),
    12, 28–30, 42, 47, 50, 86, 90, 113
International Swaps and Derivatives
    Association (ISDA), 9, 67–68
International trade imbalances, 53,
    89–92
Ireland, 4, 30, 50, 53, 105
Italian city-states, 36–7
Italy, 50

Japan, 40, 45, 88,
JP Morgan Chase,
    9, 20

Keynes, John Maynard, 75,78
Kindleberger, Charles, 2, 110
Knight, Frank, 51, 74,
Knorr Cettina, Karen, 58, 111

Latin America, 4, 50
Lazards, 38
Leeson, Nick, 58
Lehman Brothers, 20, 22, 40, 48, 69,
    97, 101, 104
Lenin, Vladimir, 44, 46,
leverage, 20–22, 108
liberalism, 73–84
Lloyds Insurance, 40, 112
Long Term Capital Management,
    (LTCM), 63, 103

Malaysia, 30
Mandlebrot, B., 76
market ideology, 7, 49, 73–84
market Utopianism, 7, 79–81
markets; and actor network theory, 68;
    disputed claims to efficiency, 21, 26,
    61–64, 69, 76, 92–93; failure,
    73–84, 92–97; limits to rationality,
    2–3, 57–64, 69; importance of
    people (social actors) within, 3;
    importance of politics and culture,
    2–3, 9–13, 55–70, 76–77;
    significance of trust, 11–12, 31–32;
    social construction of, 67–70
Marx, Karl, 43,

McKenzie, Duncan, 57, 75, 110
mathematics and finance, 20–21,
 61–64, 75, 103
Medici family, 36
Mexico, 45
Middle East, 35
money, 34–35, 41
Moodys, 9, 24, 112
moral hazard, 104–5

Nation-states and access to credit,
 14–5, 26–28, 36–9, 47–48, 52–3,
 64–67
NASDAQ, 9,
Netherlands, 37
New York Stock Exchange, 9, 58,
normative reform of capital markets,
 95–97
Northern Rock Building
 Society, 22

open-outcry markets, 9, 58–59

payment services, 15
Peruzzi family, 36
Pimco (Pacific Investment
 Management Company), 9
Pixley, Jocelyn, 57, 59, 61,
 77–79, 111,
Polanyi, Karl, 82–83, 111
Portugal, 50, 53
Prussia, 47
public policy issues for finance, 7,
 42–43, 50, 64–67, 85–106
public policy failure, 97–105

ratings agencies, 9, 24, 31, 46
regulation; as an organic part of
 finance, 12, 28–33, 42, 99;
 complex global, national and local
 levels, 102; cycles of regulation
 and deregulation, 11, 29, 43;
 definition of, 13, 31, 73; failure
 of, 97–103; public and private, 9,
 23–24, 31, 35, 42–43, 86;
 regulatory capitalism, 13, 23, 99

Reinhart, Carmen, and Rogoff,
 Kenneth, 12, 49, 110,
Reuters, 9
risk and uncertainty, 7, 12, 21–26,
 29–30, 40, 51, 54, 69–70, 74–75,
 86, 92; 96–97, 100–101, 103, 108
Rothschild family, 38, 47
Rumsfeld, Donald, 75
Russia, 63

Schumpeter, Joseph, 6, 44
Securities Exchange Commission
 (SEC), 31
securitization, 18–22, 25, 103, 108
Shackle, George, 75
Shanhai stock exchange, 39
shareholder value, 46
Shiller, Robert, 78–79, 111
Silk Road, 35
Smith, Adam, 72
social differentiation, 60, 62, 82–84,
 86, 93–94, 105–106, 109
sociology; approach to economic
 life, 10–13, 34, 67–70;
 perspectives on finance, 1–2,
 6–7, 10–13, 32, 54, 59, 62.
 67–70, 77–84, 86–87, 93–94,
 105–106
Soros Fund Management, 9,
South Korea, 45
sovereign debt crises, 5, 11, 47–48,
 50, 53, 63, 87
Standard and Poors, 9, 24
statistical issues in finance, 56, 61–64,
 76, 84
stock exchanges, 9, 39, 58
Stockholm, 38
Stockholms Banco, 38
sub-prime mortgage crisis in US,
 21–22, 25, 29, 52, 109
Sweezy, Paul, 43
Sydney, 9

Taleb, Nassim Nicholas, 51
Tokyo, 9, 39
traders, 57–61

trading rooms, 55, 57–61
Turner, Adair, 15, 110

UK, 22, 31, 37, 45, 52,
 96, 99
USA, 1, 5, 12, 20, 25, 28,
 30–31, 41–42, 45, 50, 52–3,
 88–91, 93, 99–102
US Federal Reserve, 9, 30–31,
 41–42, 52, 65, 74, 78, 85,
 98, 113
US Senate Banking Committee, 66

Vancouver, 38

Wall Street, 102
Wall Street crash of 1929, 4, 20, 52
Weber, Max, 34, 111
Wolf, Martin, 90–91, 111
Woolley, Paul, 95–97, 111
World Bank, 12, 42
World Trade Organization
 (WTO), 68

Zurich, 9